CHRYSALIS

Volume 1

PUBLISHER, David B. Eller
EDITORIAL BOARD, John L. Hitchcock, *Chair*
SERIES EDITOR, Carol S. Lawson
ART EDITOR, Alice B. Skinner
COVER DESIGN AND ART, Laury Egan
SENIOR EDITOR, Robert Lawson
ASSOCIATE EDITOR, Susanna van Rensselaer
FICTION EDITOR, Phoebe Loughrey

♦

ILLUSTRATION, VERSO, Dian McCarthy

GOLD FROM ASPIRIN
Spiritual Views on Chaos and Order from Thirty Authors

EDITED BY CAROL S. LAWSON

CHRYSALIS BOOKS
Imprint of the Swedenborg Foundation
West Chester, Pennsylvania

The *Chrysalis Reader* is a book series that examines themes
related to the universal quest for wisdom. Inspired
by the Swedenborg Foundation journal *Chrysalis*, each volume
presents original short stories, essays, poetry, and art exploring
the spiritual dimensions of a chosen theme. Works
are selected by the series editor. For information
on future themes or submission of original writings, contact
Carol S. Lawson, Editor,
Route 1, Box 184, Dillwyn, Virginia 23936.

◆

This first *Chrysalis Reader* is also Number 3, Volume IX,
Chrysalis: Journal of the Swedenborg Foundation, Winter 1994 / 1995 issue.

© 1995 by the Swedenborg Foundation
All rights reserved.
No part of this book may be reproduced or transmitted in any form
or by any means, electronic or mechanical, including photocopying, recording,
or any information storage or retrieval system, without prior permission
from the publisher, except in the case of brief quotations
embodied in critical articles and reviews.
Printed and bound in the United States of America

Library of Congress Cataloging-in-Publication Data

Gold from aspirin: spiritual views on chaos and order,
from thirty authors / Carol S. Lawson, editor
p. cm. — (Chrysalis reader: v. 1)
"Also number 3, volume IX, Chrysalis: journal
of the Swedenborg Foundation, winter 1994 / 1995 issue"—T.p. verso.
Includes bibliographical references.
ISBN 0-87785-225-1
1. American literature—20th century
2. Spiritual life—Literary collections.
3. Swedenborg, Emanuel, 1688–1772—Influence.
4. Mysticism—Literary ccollections.
5. Order—Literary collections.
I. Lawson, Carol S. II. Series
PS509.S62G65 1995

CHRYSALIS BOOKS

Imprint of the Swedenborg Foundation
320 North Church Street
West Chester, Pennsylvania 19380

♦ CONTENTS ♦

FOREWORD — vii
DAVID B. ELLER

PREFACE — ix
ROBERT H. KIRVEN

🍁 INTRODUCTION
And, Once Again, Order — 3
ALICE B. SKINNER

🍁 PART I: NATURE'S PATTERNS

A Dark Eye in the Atlantic — 11
FRANK LEONARD

Settling into My Name (poem) — 15
ZOË LANDALE

Nature's Patterns — 17
ANNE B. PERRY

Linneaus's Apprentice:
Artifice and the Tree of Life — 23
JUDY PURDY

The High Price of Order — 30
WICKHAM SKINNER

The Decoy Carver (poem) — 37
EUGENE HOLLAHAN

Interventions — 39
J. S. LINTON

Motion: A Spectrum of Order — 47
GREGORY L. BAKER

The River (poem) — 57
SUSAN FLAGG POOLE

A Brief Moment of Confusion
about the Nature of God — 59
WALTER R. CHRISTIE

I'm Told (poem) — 79
TOM O'GRADY

🍁 PART II: SPIRITUAL LIVING

Spiritual Eldering:
Coming to Terms with Mortality — 83
ZALMAN SCHACHTER

Everything in Its Place — 89
BARBARA CASEY

Offerings of Chaos (poem) — 93
ROSE ROSBERG

Stopping at Ewa — 95
PENNY PAGLIARO

Is Good Citizenship
Dual Citizenship? — 105
GEORGE F. DOLE

Whaling Blood (poem) — 111
ROBERT LAWSON

The Water's Edge — 113
ISRAEL REA

Return to the Summer
House (poem) — 124
KATE CHENEY CHAPPELL

The Problem with Evil — 127
MICHAEL D. PHILLIPS

To Live the Faith — 135
SONIA SHAH

Molten Transformations (poem) — 141
JUDITH DOHERTY QUANN

🍁 PART III: HEAVENLY SECRETS

Indian Creation Stories — 145
BECKY CONDIT

The Cosmic Order — 149
WILSON VAN DUSEN

Bryonia, Belladonna, My Father — 153
NAOMI GLADISH SMITH

The Letter — 159
LEE F. SNYDER

Ice Fishing — 165
PETER BETHANIS

Meaning Out of Chaos — 169
JOHN L. HITCHCOCK

Physical Devotions (poem) — 180
EDWARD BARATTA

FOREWORD

Chaos, Order, and Spiritual Growth: Gold from Aspirin

◆

THIS BOOK IS ABOUT CHAOS, ORDER, AND THE PROCESS of reclaiming order out of chaos. This re-ordering is a difficult task; it may indeed require much aspirin every time an individual undertakes it, yet the process promotes individual development. You will thus find that chaos/order are not necessarily a pair of opposites, but that chaos provides a favorable condition to create new order. By repeated attempts to regenerate the spirit, we may eventually achieve that celestial state symbolized by gold as described by the Swedish mystic Emanuel Swedenborg.

These stories and articles are written by people, who, time and time again, have sought meaning and spiritual growth out of chaotic circumstances. Their works have been arranged in a sequence that reflects Swedenborg's interpretation of spiritual growth, *natural* (Nature's Patterns: stories and articles related especially to the material and natural world), *spiritual* (Spiritual Living: stories and articles that explore love for the neighbor and an understanding of the world of spirit surrounding us), and *celestial* (Heavenly Secrets: stories and articles concomitantly related to love of the divine and love of sharing one's talents).

The authors presented here view life as a journey toward higher understanding. They stand ready in these pages to share with fellow wayfarers their transforming and illuminating experiences and their knowledge of the journey. In the same spirit of sharing, the Swedenborg Foundation publishes *Chrysalis Books,* such as this book, as a contribution to the universal quest for spiritual wisdom.

—DAVID B. ELLER, *Publisher*

♦ PREFACE ♦

Chrysalis Transformed

♦

INDIVIDUALLY AND COLLECTIVELY, these stories, poems, and essays have come from various kinds of chaos into their present order. There is a vast gulf between a writer's chaos—ideas, terms, thoughts, connections, and images—and an order by which typographic conventions convey an author's thoughts, emotions, and conceptions to a reader through the printed page. Another gulf separates a pile of unedited typescripts on an editor's desk, beside the red pen and aspirin bottle, from a selected, edited, organized, and sequenced collection of authors' writings.

Emanuel Swedenborg, the eighteenth-century Swedish mystic who visited real hells and real heavens, also wrote and edited enough books that his opinion bears weight in this area. He saw chaos as a necessary stage in the process of getting things done.

> Before anything is brought back into order, it is quite normal for it to be brought first into a kind of confusion, a virtual chaos. In this way, things that fit together badly are severed from each other; and, when they have been severed, then God arranges them in order.[1]

In another passage, he compared the religious thoughts of a person beginning a process of spiritual growth to

> some undigested and uncompounded mass, and to a kind of chaos. But this is to the end that they may be reduced to order.[2]

Pragmatically, things in order work. Things in disorder do not. Swedenborg, an engineer and mechanic, as well as a theoretical scientist, liked things working. After a remarkable series of spiritual experiences that led him from science to theology, he came to see not only that order is good, but also that Good is Order. God is order itself and acts only in orderly ways.

The relationship between chaos and order, however, is more

complex than that between darkness and light. *Chaos is not the opposite of order:* it is the potential from which order may arise; it harbors an order or orders not yet discerned, and it is the limit which order cannot violate and still be order.

This interplay of order and chaos has been peculiarly evident in the emergence of the present volume. The number and quality of submissions pushed the selection process for our former journal *Chrysalis* toward chaos. At the same time, a commonplace natural phenomenon played out a remarkable parable.

The *Chrysalis* editor was given a milkweed branch, which had a large green-and-black caterpillar on one of its leaves.

It was at that time that the difficulties confronting the journal had become most acute. Then, on the morning of the day that the notion of *Chrysalis* evolving into a book—a book placing a larger number of essays in conversation with one another—revealed a new order which resolved a chaotic patch of difficulties, the black chrysalis, decorated with a line of gold dots, became transparent, displaying within itself a folded pattern of orange and black. By noon upon that very day when the *Chrysalis* journal became a series of books titled the *Chrysalis Reader,* a monarch butterfly emerged from its chrysalis.

—ROBERT H. KIRVEN

Robert H. Kirven is the author of *Angels in Action,* a director of the Swedenborg Foundation, and a leading scholar of Swedenborg in the United States.

Notes

1. Swedenborg, Emanuel. *Arcana Coelestia.* New York: Swedenborg Foundation, 1984. Paragraph 842[3].

2. Dole, George. *A View from Within.* New York: Swedenborg Foundation, 1985. p. 77.

GOLD FROM ASPIRIN

> There are three vertical levels in every individual: natural, spiritual, and heavenly.
> —SWEDENBORG

ALICE B. SKINNER

INTRODUCTION
And, Once Again, Order

♦

Perhaps there was a time when the world was well-ordered and serene.

> The year's at the spring
> And the day's at the morn;
> Morning's at seven;
> The hillside's dew-pearled;
> The lark's on the wing;
> The snail's on the thorn;
> God's in his heaven—
> All's right with the world![1]

Humans helped to pattern creation.

Farms, it seems to me, are the closest analogue to the Creation we have. All our mythologies tell us that God or the gods made an ordered universe from incomprehensible chaos. Equipped with less than divine powers, we make smaller ordered universes out of the vast, teeming complexity of nature. Millions of animal species are more than we can handle, so we keep cows, horses, sheep, pigs. . . . A farm is in nature and of nature but contrary to nature; it is our small gear that meshes with the greater one of creation.[2]

Lennard, Erica. *Giardini Giusti, Verona* (left). Photograph. Washington, D.C.: Govinda Gallery.
[1] Browning, Robert. Pippa Passes. In *Pauline. Paracelsus. Pippa Passes. King Victor and King Charles.* New York: Thomas Y. Crowell & Company. pp. 192–193. ll. 221–228.
[2] Kimber, Robert. *Upcountry*. New York: Lyons & Burford. 1991. pp. 54–55.

ORDER APPEALS to us—whether in refrigerators or on desks, in the body politic or in our daily lives and relationships. Tidiness makes the world seem predictable and manageable. Disorder spawns uncertainty and misery, yet maintaining order is always a struggle. However fine the organization of—things, time, people—it tends to disintegrate into dishes that need to be done, bills that should have been paid, or even shattered relationships.

James McGarrell[3]

---

[3]McGarrell, James. *A Fine Excess with Chardin Quotation.* Oil on canvas, 1978/1979. Tucson: The University of Arizona Museum of Art. Museum purchase with funds provided by The Edward J. Gallagher, Jr., Memorial Fund.

IS TURBULENCE an inevitable fact of life? Does it serve a purpose?

> Without the violence, the major shift,
> The shudder of the earth's foundations torn,
> Without the great upheaval which could lift
> That fiery core, it would not have been born,
> And yet when chaos cooled, this land was here,
> Absolute and austere—
> Then, not before,
> It snowed.
> Later, by centuries and centuries,
> The saving water flowed,
> The grass arrived, dark little trees.
> After a terrible and rending war,
> This land took on its fearful peace,
> After, and not before.[4]

PERHAPS CHAOS is an aspect of the divine design, in lives as well as in nature, a means of sloughing off discordant elements so that a new order can evolve.

Before anything is brought back into order, it is quite normal for it to be brought first into a kind of confusion, a virtual chaos. In this way, things that fit together badly are severed from each other; and when they have been severed, then God arranges them in order.[5]

---

[4]Sarton, May. Without the Violence. In *Collected Poems (1930–1973)*.
New York: W.W. Norton & Co., Inc. p. 148.
[5]Swedenborg, Emanuel. *Arcana Coelestia*. Paragraph no. 842.3. In George Dole,
A View from Within. New York: Swedenborg Foundation, 1985. p. 77.

TIMES OF UPHEAVAL teach us to clarify what is important and to seek new paths.

> In a dark time, the eye begins to see,
> I meet my shadow in the deepening shade;
> I hear my echo in the echoing wood—
> A lord of nature weeping to a tree . . .
> What's madness but nobility of soul
> At odds with circumstance? The day's on fire!
> I know the purity of pure despair,
> My shadow pinned against a sweating wall.
> That place among the rocks—is it a cave,
> Or winding path? The edge is what I have.[7]

---

[6] El Greco (Domenikos Theotokopoulos). *The Repentant St. Peter.* Oil on canvas, c. 1600–1604 or later. Washington, D.C.: The Phillips Collection.
[7] Roethke, Theodore. In a Dark Time. In *The Collected Poems of Theodore Roethke.* New York: Doubleday Anchor Books, 1975. p. 231. ll. 1–4, 7–12.

WE DISCOVER PATTERNS that communicate new visions of order.

> Again the oak, bare, stripped and barren, brings
> More confirmation to the heart than Spring's
> Returning green; more courage to refind
> winter-bones of spirit unobscured
> By summer-flesh of leaves. The troubled mind
> After the Fall's deception, reassured—
> After the wind, after the winter storm—
> By deep return to discipline of form.[8]

Childe Hassam[9]

BEGINNING at the edges, following winding paths, we recognize new possibilities in ourselves and new approaches to the situations we encounter.

> The great sea has set me in motion,
> set me adrift,
> moving me like a weed in a river.
>
> The sky and the strong wind
> have moved the spirit inside me
> till I am carried away
> trembling with joy.[10]

---

[8]Lindberg, Anne Morrow. Winter Tree. In *The Unicorn and Other Poems, 1935–1955*. New York: Vintage Books. 1972. p. 62.
[9]Hassam, Childe. *Bathing Pool, Appledore*. Oil on canvas, twentieth century. Museum of Fine Arts, Boston. Ernest Wadsworth Longfellow Fund.
[10]Uvavnuk. The Great Sea Has Set Me in Motion. In Stephen Mitchell, ed. *The Enlightened Heart*. New York: Harper & Row. 1989. p. 123.

John Constable[11]

RENEWED order fits us to root and grow in more nourishing soil.

> Blessed are the man and the woman
> who have grown beyond their greed
> and have put an end to their hatred
> and no longer nourish illusions.
> But they delight in the way things are
> and keep their hearts open, day and night.
> They are like trees planted near flowing rivers,
> which bear fruit when they are ready.
> Their leaves will not fall or wither.
> Everything they do will succeed.[12]

Alice Skinner, president of the Swedenborg Foundation, is a student of women's lives, who tries to limit chaos in her home on the coast of Maine.

---

[11] Constable, John. *On the River Stour.* Oil on canvas, c. 1834–1837. Washington, D.C.: The Phillips Collection.
[12] Psalm 1. In Stephen Mitchell, ed. *The Enlightened Heart.* New York: Harper & Row. 1989. p. 5.

PART I
Nature's Patterns

◆

We are born
on the natural level,
and our natural talents
increase
with our factual learning
—all the way
to that peak
of discernment
we call rationality.

—ADAPTED FROM SWEDENBORG

◆ FRANK S. LEONARD ◆

A Dark Eye in the Atlantic

◆

I WAS BROUGHT TO SEMICONSCIOUSNESS, midway between sleep and waking, by something—something violent and insistent, something from outside the room. I have awakened in many hotels, with so many internal demands stripping me from sleep, that now, when first perceptions came, I was disoriented. Bangkok? Los Angeles? Frankfurt? Our home, Cambridge? No. Jennifer and I were in our cottage in Maine. There it was again, violently insistent. Wide-awake now, sitting upright, trying not to disturb Jennifer, I listened. Again it came. Consciousness locked on the source—the wind.

I slipped quietly out of bed and downstairs. The November early gray light filtered into the house through windows almost completely coated with ice and snow. I glimpsed snow horizontally streaming past. The wind was building and, as it did, it palpably shifted the house. With visibility to the outside effectively blocked, I felt I was in the hold of a ship, blindly sensing the early movements of a vast storm. A wind had been formed in a dark eye over the North Atlantic. Despite scientific weather forecasts to the contrary, "a light dusting," my blood sensed the fury in that dark eye. It would be a dangerous and awe-full day; a day as far removed from the artificial order of my work life as is imaginable; a day reeling from the punches of a Nor'easter. The way we normally experience things is nullified when we are reduced to elementals. Like all extremes, it can throw my ordered life into sharp relief.

The Lydian stone, consisting of the mineral basalt and called a *touchstone*, was used by alchemists to test the purity of gold and silver by the streak left on the stone. This day might become a touchstone to test the purity of the life I had chosen, the work I do.

I went about the ministrations of a winter morning in Maine:

Skinner, Wickham, *Woodpile*. Photograph, Maine, 1995.

wood stove refilled, teakettle on top of the stove, cats fed, coffee ground, a slice of bread with honey, the temperature outside checked. 30° F. It was still very early. I tried to be quiet, in my own way—a bull in a closet. The storm had started only a little while ago. I could still see cracks between the boards in the deck. The storm had started as sleet, sheathing vertical surfaces in ice.

The wind was howling from the NNE with gusts of 40 MPH. Like water, the wind would break upon the house in waves, the spruces and birches bowing toward the ground in obeisance. Because of the wind, the snow was actually falling *up* at times, great swirls obscured visibility through small portholes I had scraped in the windows. Wind-sculpted drifts were already forming on the south side of the house, precursor of the day's (r)evolution.

After breakfast I put on winter storm gear and stepped out. The contrast to the muted gray protection of the cottage was stunningly acute, like walking from a quiet hotel room into a conference room frothing with high-tension executives. Nature, like those self-made executives, was out to test this man to see what he was made of. But the testing here was of an inhuman kind, the test of Nature.

Under the force of the driving snow, I was almost blind. I checked to make sure the wood bin by the back door was full—an unnecessary check because I knew perfectly well it was. It was a check, though, mixed with reassurance and comfort, of being in a situation against which, and for which, we had prepared.

I found my thoughts returning like swallows to a barn—to my work, my clients. As I walked to the road—so desolate—my mind returned to Australia and the assignment I had returned from six days before. It was 1 AM the next day in Melbourne. It is dissembling to work intensely with a group of people and then leave. I often wonder if they think about me as much as I think about them.

But bowing into the fierce wind, I walked across the field to the "office"—a small garage, office, and guest apartment. The office consists of a 10-by-12-foot room, desks, computer, telephone, facsimile, files, and a wood stove. I threw off my snow gear, lit a fire, and sat at my desk. I was in the midst of preparing a presentation for a global conference on corporate strategy. The draft was on the desk. I jotted down a wisp of a thought I had had at breakfast.

There are very few moments when I am free from the order I impose on myself for work. My job is to help people reach higher levels of understanding. But all ascents carry the possibility of a fall. I carry a burden of responsibility for the ideas I craft. I am always testing, refining, changing the concepts, models, and language. I put the paper down, spin away from the wood stove, and gaze at opaque, ice-coated windows.

The wind, snarling, swiped again at the building. The fury of the storm had grown. The electric lights flickered, a power outage was likely. I looked at the telephone. Should I call my answering service at 7 AM in the morning to see if any calls had come in from Europe? No. The rising wind crowded out all such thoughts.

I went upstairs to the small apartment. The windows were clear, but I couldn't see the ocean, a mere 80 feet away. The blowing snow obscured all but the first line of spruces. A lone gull, a herring gull, *Larus argentatus,* was trying to fight his way against the wind, making headway but only at sharp oblique angles to the wind. He veered into the snowy inferno endlessly flying.

The power went off at 10:15 AM, a flicker and then nothing. It is so strange, when feeding off this vast man-made network of utilities, they just stop. We normally have no idea how or where the break is. Somewhere, the order of the storm superimposes itself on the order of the power company. A break in the technological system leaves me with contradictory emotions: first, a self-assuredness it will soon be fixed, a confidence in the masters of the system; second, a barely perceptible feeling of vulnerability and dependence-at-risk.

Our cottage is more self-sustaining than most. The water pump is the only victim to the power outage. The wood stoves are more than capable for heat, and, thanks to Jennifer, candles abound for light. Our meals could be cooked on the bottled-gas stove or on the wood stove. The storm reached its zenith right after noon—winds gusting to 60 MPH, snowdrifts building to three feet, roads impassable. My entire attention was focused on maintaining shelter and safety. As the storm grew, no further thoughts of politics or economics barged in, no concerns about the Far East industrial dynamics. The social artifice had melted away under Nature's rage.

Life returns to its simplest form in the face of such chaos: fire, water, light, food, wind. Even when the storm subsided, when would we get power back? How long would our food last? When would the roads be cleared? Future goals, predictability, long-range plans become mockeries of themselves. They imply an inflated degree of control, a linearity. Their usefulness, now, had evaporated under the leveling effect of the storm.

This vast storm reflected my own psychic state. To me, my work is not like an inner calm day; it is a great storm of ideas, emotion, and action. Every moment contains an endless number of possibilities. I am always caught between possibility and choice, problem and answer. Like this storm, my work entails a vast amount of energy, often artificially created and sustained. Sometimes *I* am the dark eye of the storm, sweeping into my client's world. Sometimes I am swept along with them. But all of our confidence, our composure, can be taken away in a moment. "Knowledge" is the cloak I wear, and it is often a thin wrap.

Nature forced us into a situation in which there was no time for self-reflection, no array of options, no questions. Just maintaining warmth, light, and food kept us huddled on the threshold of chaos. As the afternoon sank upon us, the steel-gray water, finally visible, whipped by the wind, contrasted with a snowscaped land.

In mid-afternoon, without any lessening in snow or wind, the storm's anger had been breached. The dark eye was slouching away into the North Atlantic. I went back to the office as the early night began to encroach on us. I put more wood in the stove, checked windows and doors, and had one more look at the wood pile to assuage my lurking doubts. I walked out to the road: no plows or cars. I shoveled out the back door one more time. Activities sprung of necessity, not of choice, moved me. Back inside with Jennifer, lighting a fire in the fireplace, we could only smile. Tomorrow would be different. We would make plans and renew once more our tenuous world of order.

Frank Leonard is an international business consultant specializing in global manufacturing companies. He lives with his wife, Jennifer, in Cambridge, Massachusetts, and Tenants Harbor, Maine.

ZOË LANDALE

Settling Into My Name

WHEN I AM settled into my name,
bringer of order,
I am immensely powerful
The trick is, simultaneity
without rushing
weave one action into another
so I have a morning without seam
my daughter in her yellow sleeper
plus bear plus blanket
nested in a sunny kitchen
I have learned to restore harmony
secretively & without end
as though the washing machine
started itself,
counters wiped themselves
dishes stack as toast cooks

I guess you don't get much time for handwork
what with your writing & all
Aunt Rose says
ninety-two & always looping wool
into colored symmetry
or making fine lace curtains & tablecloths
I look at her as if she's said something
exotic
see myself for an instant pulling more hours from the day,
finished pieces I could hang, wear
keep overnight without melting
or being eaten
tangible art
which would stay
still

Meaning is found
in the everyday patterns
of the natural world.

♦ ANNE B. PERRY ♦

Nature's Patterns

♦

The earth does not withhold, it is generous enough,
The truths of the earth continually wait, they are not so concealed either.
They are calm, subtle, untransmissible by print,
They are imbued through all things conveying themselves willingly,
Conveying a sentiment and invitation, I utter and I utter,
I speak not, yet if you hear me not of what avail am I to you?
—WALT WHITMAN

THINK ABOUT BUDS ON A TREE OR SHRUB, inconspicuous there in the axils of the leaves, hugging the twigs, waiting. In those buds are next year's leaves and flowers, and the potential for leaves and flowers for the following year, and the year after that. The buds call to mind those Eastern European wooden dolls which when opened contain a smaller doll, and so on until the tiniest doll is found. But there is something missing here—the element of time. In looking at Nature's patterns, we can look at two dimensions on flat surfaces, or three-dimensional solids, or four dimensions that include the passage of time. Patterns through time become cycles—life cycles or seasonal cycles or galactic cycles.

IN MYTH AND CULTURE, cycles have been depicted as circles. Ancient Celts lived in round houses as do nomads of today. The roundness can symbolize the cycle of lives lived there. The Celts added a circle to their cross. Native Americans bring circles into their lives in many ways—ceremony, dance, medicine, meetings.

Pen-and-ink drawings by Nancy Marstaller, 1995.

Can postmodern humans also learn to live symbolically, recapturing our circular creativity that is so often trapped in linear literalism?

THINK ABOUT A STONE rounded by moving water, its journey from mother bedrock through tumbling waterfall to rest on a sandy shore. Native Americans are always alert for special stones called *wotais* in which they see significant images. In this piece of Mother Earth, they find parallels to guide their lives. The roundness of a water-worn stone can be compared to a person's progress through life. As we live through the rough times, we lose our sharp edges and are better able to "roll with the punches." In ancient Britain and America stones were arranged in circles for celestial ceremonies and calculations.

WHAT ABOUT THE CIRCLE as represented in living things? The most primitive life forms had radial symmetry; that is, any line through the center creates mirror images on either side and a vertical axis runs through the mouth in the center. Later radial symmetry became one of life's great repeated patterns found in starfish, sea anemones, and sand dollars. In three dimensions the radial pattern becomes a sphere and sometimes a concentric sphere as in onions. Picture ourselves and our experiences of the world as spheres with dots at the centers. The surfaces of the spheres are our egos where our conscious selves interface with others and the natural world. The centers of the spheres are our psyches, our real selves evolving. The centers are dots with no dimensions in space or time. Our job is to find that center and adjust the way we define ourselves to it, not just to the way others define us.

WE KNOW OF PI, the figure (3.1416 . . .) representing the ratio of the circumference of a circle to the minute-hand of its radius. Even when figured to thousands of decimal places, it will not come out even. It is one of the remaining mysteries of mathematics.

Long ago in biology class I learned that the main difference between something that is living and that which is nonliving is its level of organization. A molecule of salt is simplicity itself when compared to a molecule of an enzyme in a mouse's body. The ultimate in complexity seemed to be the DNA in every living cell which carries the code for development of each living thing. I wondered then and now what inner truths I might draw from this knowledge. Is our world forever fighting entropy through creation and recreation of life? Do nonliving things organize themselves into patterns too? What force is the strange attractor behind the creation of order in Nature?

A vine winds its way around a pole as it reaches for sunlight. The same spiral pattern is found in twisted tree trunks and innumerable other plants. One of the great riddles of botany is the consistency of those spirals. The medieval mathematician Fibonacci discovered a number series that was later named after him. The Fibonacci series (1, 1, 2, 3, 5, 8, 13, 21, 34, 55, 89 . . .) consists of numbers that progress by adding the previous two numbers. As the numbers increase, the ratio approaches the "golden mean" used by the Greek architects to achieve the marvelous balance of their buildings (1:1.618). The series is also found throughout nature, notably in plants. In phyllotaxis, leaf arrangement around a stem, the numbers of superimposed rows of spirals, clockwise and counterclockwise, are always adjacent Fibonacci numbers. You can count the spirals most easily on a pine cone or a sunflower.

SPIRALS ARE SEEN in galaxies, in snails, and in our lives. The spiral path leads us to the center, or outward and upward on new levels each time we come around. I have from time to time had the feeling I have been in a certain place before in my life but am now observing it from a different level.

THE CADUCEUS OF HERMES consisted of two serpents twining around a staff. Their opposite spirals represented the union of opposing forces, as well as balance and equilibrium. Today it is the symbol of the medical profession. It may not escape your notice that the very same pattern is found in DNA, the substance of every living cell that governs the development of the whole. The zipper-like quality of the double helix allows it to separate and come back together. Duality is a necessary part of spiritual growth.

RADIAL SYMMETRY worked for most creatures living in the sea, but, as they emerged onto the land, a different body shape was required. A new pattern took precedence: bilateral symmetry. A plane through the body divides it into two opposite parts or mirror images, to which may be added legs for better locomotion. It started with worms and fish, then with arthropods, amphibians, and reptiles, and later with birds and mammals. Insects in particular should be noted for their successful versions of bilateral symmetry, as well as plants for their opposite leaf arrangement.

Are our own two opposite sides equal? Brain research has shown that the right and left hemispheres operate differently. The left hemisphere governs our right side and specializes in language (literalism), reasoning (positivism), and analysis. The right hemisphere governs our left side and is imaginative, holistic, intuitive, and nonverbal. The two hemispheres are connected by a complex cable of nerves, and, if all goes well, they work together. But Left often overcomes Right and is favored by the hard-edged, rationalistic climate that prevails in today's Western societies.

A whole tree appears bilaterally symmetrical and yields a fascinating analogy to the brain. Think of the deep root system as the intuitive right brain and the upper branches as the enlightened, reasoning left brain. We—and the tree—need both to become whole.

As we have only limited senses with which to perceive the natural world, we must sometimes use scientific instruments to help us "see" patterns. We now know that patterns that we can see with our own senses are reflections of the patterns of the basic particles of matter. Each molecule of a crystal of amethyst is linked up in precisely the same shape as the crystal you can see. Furthermore the DNA in every cell of your body knows exactly what your whole body should look like. Nothing is too small to show a pattern of the whole. That is what holograms are about. The notion that the whole is present in all of its parts was late in gaining credence, and we are finally getting it together. We are part of the Universe and as such reflect every part thereof.

Rachel Carson said in *The Sense of Wonder,* "Those who contemplate the beauty of the earth find reserves that will endure as long as life lasts." Appreciation of nature's patterns, from molecular to celestial and through all time, is a path to spiritual renewal.

Anne B. Perry holds a bachelor's degree in zoology from Smith College and a master's degree in science education from Framingham State University. She taught environmental education in the Boston area before retiring to the coast of Maine. When not doing volunteer work for town and community, she contemplates meaningful patterns of nature.

Readings

Carson, Rachel. *The Sense of Wonder.* Illustrated by Charles Pratt. New York: Harper & Row, 1965.

Howell, Alice O. *The Dove in the Stone: Finding the Sacred in the Commonplace.* Wheaton, Illinois: Theosophical Publishing House, 1988.

Matthews, Boris, trans. *Herder Symbol Dictionary.* Willamette, Illinois: Chiron Publications, 1987.

Murphy, Pat and William Neil. *By Nature's Design.* San Francisco: Chronicle Books, 1993.

Whitman, Walt. *Leaves of Grass.* New York: Bantam Books, 1892 and 1983.

♦ *JUDY PURDY* ♦

Linnaeus's Apprentice
Artifice and the Tree of Life

♦

WE ALL DO IT. EVERYDAY. To one extreme or another. Or at least we try. My boss is compelled to do it. Engaged in his own private, never-ending battle, he is forever trying to bring order out of chaos. His desk, the epitome of orderliness, is the antithesis of mine, which is characteristically littered with piles of files, day-old phone messages, and stale cups of tea. In contrast, his is nearly bereft of paperwork and ornamentation—every pencil is sharpened, every pen in perfect alignment, every paperclip in its place.

His propensity for order provides impetus for good-natured pranks, especially during staff meetings where the person sitting next to him might lean close to his desk and slyly "disorganize" those neat rows of writing tools. Then the staff watches as he unconsciously realigns things until we can no longer suppress our laughter, and he becomes wise to our antics.

Although few of us are as excessive as my boss, all of us develop hierarchies to handle the barrage of daily information. What must we remember? What to forget? What to tuck away for future reference?

As a college senior, I was to learn a time-honored system for ordering the vast world of plants. I now recognize it as one of the more valuable tools I acquired as a science major. At the time it was just part of the curriculum. Any well-educated biology major took a course on systematics. Listed as field botany in the college catalog, trial by fire might have been a more apt name for the class on the taxonomic system of nomenclature devised by the eighteenth-

---

Following a field trip to Lapland, Carolus Linnaeus (1707–1778) posed for his portrait in the dress of an eighteenth-century Laplander. (Hunt Institute for Botanical Documentation. Pittsburgh, Carnegie Mellon University.)

century Swedish botanist, Carolus Linnaeus (neé Carl von Linné), who, incidentally, was a cousin of Swedenborg, the Swedish scientist, statesman, and seer.

An invaluable tool for bringing order to the world of trees, shrubs, and flowers, Linnaeus's system rapidly gained acceptance in the scientific community and became *the* system for naming and thus ordering all living and once-living organisms—from Jurassic dinosaurs to relative newcomers, such as orchids.

As botany students, we learned that "real" taxonomy in the plant world is based on reproductive parts—flowers and fruits, pistils and stamens—because they are the most invariant parts of plants, exhibiting the least variation within a species from one generation to the next. Because leaves, stems, and roots are highly variable, they shed little light on botanical relationships and are considered artificial characteristics in taxonomy.

Dr. Carole Markle, the high priestess of plant classification at Earlham College, ran her class like a drill sergeant. We were only permitted to use *Gray's Manual of Botany*, the botanist's bible for flora of central and northeastern United States and Canada. Our mission was to collect, identify, and preserve herbarium specimens of flowering plants but, under the circumstances, it was more like a mission of search and destroy.

Armed with the tools of the trade—a trowel, notebook, pencil (pens don't write in pouring rain), masking tape labels with numbers penciled on them, magnifying lens, and vasculum (a sort of portable plant morgue for collected specimens) lined with moistened paper towels—we tackle taxonomy à la Markle.

The first order was to bag our quarry. On warm spring afternoons, about a dozen students would crowd into two college vans and set off for the Hoosier countryside with Dr. Markle at the helm. Out in the middle of nowhere, she would park the lead van, leap out, dash across a field full of flowers, and, in rapid-fire succession, point out specimens for us to collect, roots and all.

Meanwhile, we would be clambering over seats and fellow students, vasculums colliding in midair. Disentangled, we would race across fields, traverse wooded hillsides, and ford cool streams in breathless pursuit of our white-haired professor and the elusive and nameless spring wildflowers she was instructing us to dig. She would issue orders so briskly that we were hopelessly behind before we had even begun. Under the circumstances, there was no time to waste, no place for questions or complaints. Instead, we would look around in a panic, frantically trying to figure out which plants she had already pointed to, scramble to find a good specimen of our own to collect, and drop to our knees. Hurriedly we would dig, slap a masking tape label on the uprooted plant's stem, and shove it into the vasculum without taking time to appreciate its beauty. Hastily we would jot down some brief notes about habitat and location and rush off to start the process all over again. Meanwhile, Dr. Markle would have added three more specimens to the growing list. "That tall white one by the fence there, this delicate blue one, and that ground creeper over there, which has a long root," she boomed. "And make sure you get all its root."

Once back at the lab, we would set to work with the hefty manual, a hand lens, our field notes, and the nameless, already wilting specimens. Occasionally, when Dr. Markle was not looking, we worked in groups, and even then it might take an hour or more to key a specimen to genus and species. Some Fridays we would work right through dinner and on toward dusk trying to discern the true identity of one more minuscule flower. But even after we had found a name for our specimen, we were never sure if it was the right one because Dr. Markle did not correct or grade our course work until after the final exam.

Under her sink-or-swim teaching method, leaves and stems were no longer merely smooth or hairy. Hairiness now had a quality. Was it hirsute, pusillanimous, or some other new word for the condition of hairiness? A rose was no longer just a rose. Who had time to stop and smell one anyway? Forget whether it smelled as sweetly by another name unless, of course, that was an important characteristic to distinguish it from other similar species. We were playing beat the clock, and posey petals were just another taxonomic measuring stick.

Theoretically, at least, *Gray's Manual* would enable us to discover the true identify of just about any native flowering plant or fern growing from the Midwest to northeast Canada. But for flowering plants, it really only worked well if they were in bloom. Without pistils and stamens, it was next to impossible to inject order into the flora of Midwestern fields and forests. "Common" field guides used by laypersons were absolutely verboten by Dr. Markle; they were equivalent to cheating on a final exam.

After identifying our plant specimens, we pressed and dried them, preserving them on herbarium sheets for posterity, or at least until the end of the quarter. If it was hard to identify fresh flowers, it was a real challenge for beginners to find order in lifeless, dried specimens. We soon discovered that organizing chaos required healthy doses of discipline and perseverance.

For weeks we dutifully traipsed behind Dr. Markle on long treks of endurance, digging up one of everything in sight. About halfway through the quarter came the big field trip—the annual spring wildflower pilgrimage to the mountains and river valleys of Tennessee and North Carolina, one of the richest and most diverse floras in the continental United States.

The trip was filled with sudden, unplanned stops. Cruising down the highway at top speed, Dr. Markle would eye some bright spot of color, stomp on the brakes, and pull off the road. She would hop out and hurry over to what she hoped was a new or rare specimen. Moments later she might motion us to follow her and be quick about it. We would pile out, vasculums over our shoulders and trowels in our hip pockets, and crowd around to see and hear about some of America's loveliest wildflowers. At day's end, we were tired, hungry, and grumpy, with vasculums full and plant presses ready to be filled.

One evening we had planned to stay in a roadside motel, but it had fallen on hard times. So we opted for a state park, although we had no tents, just sleeping bags. Rain was forecasted, so we crawled under picnic tables until the downpour drove many of us indoors to sleep on restroom floors.

Before bed, though, we had lots of plants to identify. Like moths hovering around porch lights, clusters of students sat around picnic tables illuminated by lanterns. Our plant specimens, presses, and copies of *Gray's Manual* littered the tabletops, benches and ground around us.

Although artificial characteristics—leaf shape and arrangement, upright or climbing, upland or marsh habitat—may be considered secondary traits for snatching botanical order from the jaws of chaos, that night we learned they could be very valuable. In fact, resorting to artificial characteristics a little earlier in the identification process of one particular plant might have saved our professor from deep embarrassment.

During the day's collecting forays, fellow biology major Ann Labarre had noticed a delicate and rather obscure greenish-colored flower, and, although it was not one Dr. Markle had singled out, Ann collected it anyway. Ann was fast at keying specimens. She had worked through most of the other plants in her vasculum that evening when she decided to tackle this one. The flowers were small, the lantern light was dim, and Ann kept running into deadends with *Gray's Manual*. To make matters worse, this little greenish-white thing didn't seem to fit with any plant families we had learned so far. Occasionally she would ask Dr. Markle for an opinion on one characteristic or another. "Could it be this one?" she would query.

"Let me see it. No," Dr. Markle would answer.

"How about that one?"

"No" was the reply again.

Finally, Ann asked Dr. Markle to help her key it out. Obviously Dr. Markle had not recognized the flower immediately, or she would have halted the process right then.

Instead, we were about to witness how even a very refined system can itself create chaos. While the rest of the class looked on, the two alternately squinted at the flowers through a hand lens, while leafing through the pages of *Gray's Manual*. Dr. Markle decided to have a look at the leaves. No wonder Ann had not recognized those little flowers; her specimen was a member of the cashew family, a family we had not yet encountered. If Dr. Markle had glanced earlier at some artificial characteristics, particularly the leaves, the class would have been deprived of the vivid scene of her and Ann grabbing the Fels Naphtha soap and sprinting to the campground restroom to quickly wash off the oil of plain, old, ordinary poison ivy.

Bridges, Fidelia. *Grass and Poison Ivy*.
Watercolor on paper. Philadelphia:
The Pennsylvania Academy of the Fine Arts.
Henry D. Gilpin Fund.

BOTANISTS aren't the only ones who use classification systems to see relationships more clearly. Large or small, these systems play an important role in our daily lives. Consider a library without a Library of Congress system; instead, books are arranged randomly on shelves. No use trying to find your favorite author's newest novel unless you have time to start at the top shelf and work your way through every stack, book by book. As individuals and as a society, we rely on shared systems of organization, and those systems ought to make life easier, not harder. Even our micro systems become habits crucial to a smooth-running and predictable life. For instance, putting the car keys in the same place saves time in the midst of a tight schedule.

We could not survive as individuals, families, or communities without shared classification systems to organize our thoughts, time, and things. But despite our methods of order, there is plenty of room for creativity and compromise among people who have vastly different levels of tolerance for chaos or each other's systems. What works for you may smother me, and vice versa. My stacked-up desk system would surely drive my boss crazy just as his sterile "playing field" would hamstring me.

As cluttered and disorganized as my desk may look, it actually portrays a subtle organizational pattern. Those stacks and piles are not random; they reflect the level of order I want and need. I know what's in each pile, and I can retrieve papers quickly. Using a variation on the Linnaean theme that Dr. Markle taught, this system ignores unimportant characteristics—in this case papers—and focuses on those that matter. The "deal-with-later" stacks free up time to concentrate on more important or urgent matters.

Any workable system ought to have payoffs, and mine is no exception. I'm a science writer, not an accountant; my priorities are to maximize creative time, not to keep up-to-the-minute records of credits and debits. My system helps me organize my thoughts, set priorities, foster creativity, and seek inspiration. It relegates mundane housekeeping chores, such as filing, to creative "down" times.

Your system for keeping chaos at bay may fall somewhere between the extremes of my looseness and my boss's meticulousness. Regardless of what systems any of us use, though, situations will still arise when systems fail, as Dr. Markle unwittingly, yet poignantly, illustrated. By remaining flexible, however, we can order our systems instead of them ordering—or disordering—us.

Judy Purdy is a science writer who makes her living as director of research communications for the University of Georgia.

WICKHAM SKINNER

The High Price of Order

♦

LATE IN A SUMMER NIGHT the phone rang insistently and, finally, I staggered over to stop its irritating intrusion. On the line was one of the best students I'd ever had. Her name is Monica, and, while her good manners kept her respectful, apologetic, and friendly, Monica was mad as hops that night at the end of the second shift.

"Wick, did you really know what life in a factory is like when you talked me into taking this foreman's job at Ford? Wick, I'm in charge of twenty plastic molding machines spewing out 120,000 parts a minute. Every machine has an operator, they all need different resins that I have to order, and their parts all go different places which means piles of move orders for me to write. The machines all break down randomly and take maintenance mechanics, who have to be called and don't like it. The molds have to be replaced, the operators have to go to the bathroom at odd times, and I have to get substitutes in a hurry who hide. When the total parts produced in any ten minutes is less than 1.2 million, an awful, loud buzzer starts beeping on and off, six red lights start flashing surrounding the machine area, my boss comes shouting and cussing, and all hell breaks loose. This happened three times today, and they call it 'running red' instead of 'running black'—you've got to run black."

She ran out of breath, stopped, and then said in a low, sad voice, "This is awful, Wick."

She didn't add "and you got me into this" though I wouldn't have blamed her if she had. She was simply outraged about how animalistic life in a factory seemed in her first week on the job. As the weeks and months passed, she survived and actually came to love the pace and excitement. Her feelings about the Ford factory in her first week were entirely normal, a rational, human reaction accurately reflecting the state of most factories.

Factories are a dramatic mix of and shifts between absolute chaos and ruthless order as management desperately attempts to control thousands of variables of technology, flows of materials, parts, and assemblies, large numbers of people, and fluctuations in what customers think they want.

I once complained to a senior colleague about the declining competitive state of U.S. industry, its poor productivity, terrible quality, missed deliveries, and bad housekeeping. He said, "Well, Wick, did you ever stop to think about how miraculous it is that a factory can produce anything at all?" He is an economist and has never studied factories as I have, but he knows

Wickham Skinner. *Monica's Presses.* Pen-and-ink, 1995

statistics and so he continues, "When you think about, say, 500 people running 300 machines and work stations, producing 10,000 different parts which are made into 750 product-variations and are shipped to 700 customers who send in 7,000 orders a year, 100 engineers are writing 25 design changes a day and the orders are seasonal and the economy goes up and down and each employee has to work differently on every work order . . . Wick! Come on. Stop complaining! In theory bees can't fly, and in my mind factories are the eighth wonder of the world."

He was right, of course. Factories which work well (and most do) are amazing examples of human ability to deal with complexity and randomness. Each employee must know how and what to do every minute all week long. Work has to be available every minute and completed in time to move along somehow to the next operation. Red cars need red fenders. It takes precious time to change over machine 29 to make product "d" instead of product "k". The possibilities for error, confusion, delay, distemper, and waste of investment and cost are enormous. So how are factories managed?

The history of industrial management is a history of managers trying to prevent chaos by inventing or borrowing techniques to bring about order and control. In the beginning of industry, about 1800, textile factories were fairly simple, producing a narrow line of products. The name of the game was "mass production." Management was relatively simple. Order was maintained by strict discipline, wages were high compared to farming, and the foreman was king. Machines controlled quality and output.

By mid-nineteenth century many more industries were mechanized as the factory system incorporated more processes, products, customers, and locations. Gradually factories expanded their scope, making their own materials and more of the completed product. Textile plants, for example, started with bales of cotton and produced whole garments. Complexity grew. The fifth floor, operating independently under a foreman who liked long runs and few changeovers, made a three-year supply of part 102 for the sixth floor foreman while he ran out of part 107. Efficiency, productivity, and quality became critical for success as industrialization spread. Somehow managers had to get control. Each decade it grew harder.

The answer back then was to begin more central scheduling, process engineering, and methods engineering to standardize operations, add more inspectors, and set up cost accounting. Supervision was charged with meeting standards of workmanship, schedules, efficiency, quality, and maintenance. Supervision needed help, and, while central management was resented, it was clearly needed. The necessity of managing complexity produced a remarkable man named Frederick Taylor and "Scientific Management."

Scientific Management was based on straight-forward reductionist logic: take a product, divide it into parts, the parts into operations, the operations into the smallest steps, rationalize and improve every step, and put it all back together into a clear, written book of methods governing every operation and every operator. Instruct, train, and closely supervise the workers, and the whole factory will be not only become orderly, but efficient and profitable.

This phase of management control was only the beginning for the twentieth-century manager's obsession for reducing chaos and increasing order while ever-better regulations and controls grew even stronger. Time standards were developed by legions of industrial engineers, a new profession whose all-consuming love was efficiency. Daily reports were produced showing efficiency ratings by building, department, and every individual operator.

Productivity and efficiency helped to win the first World War, and American industry became the exemplar of the world. In the twenties, thirties, and war years of the forties methods and process engineering became even more prevalent, resulting in much more sophisticated scheduling and shop floor controls. And along came "automation," a new word for the old process of increasing mechanization of production, leaving less in the way of skill and judgment to workers. Union leaders complained that "workers are expected to leave their brains at the factory gate and just do what they are told for eight hours."

The century of ever-advancing advanced management techniques (AMTs) continues to this day with JIT (Just-in Time) and MRP (materials requirement planning), "time-based management," computer integrated manufacturing (CIM), Total Quality Management (TQM) and an alphabet soup of about twenty other techniques.

In essence, they all are set up and administered to impose order and rationalization on chaos and individuality. By and large they have worked: productivity, delivery, quality, and production flexibility is better than ever before. Chaos has been virtually eradicated, snuffed out by the computer.

Would factory life be better for Monica today? Not in most factories, if she were working at the first-line supervisory level, simply because the order is so centrally designed, controlled by fewer people, and not based on Monica's rationality. It's an imposed order and Monica, while unusually able, is not atypical when she is told how to do her job. Few of us like order imposed by order.

So there, of course, is the old rub in a new guise: managers abhor chaos, and workers abhor being controlled by anti-chaos AMTs. This theme predominates in the epic of industrial history, for about every decade there has been a wave of new AMTs, brought about by increasing competition, competitors using the same AMTs, new technology, and increasing technology.

But the price of order has been high. Many people dislike the very idea of working in a factory. The disciplines of the time clock, the foreman, the standards of output and quality, prescribed work methods, measurement systems, and frequent disregard for the individual have driven workers to resentment, unions, industrial violence, and even destruction of their machines. In reaction to ordered life in the "Satanic Mills," productivity has suffered as have quality and innovation.

The culture of the factory has driven off many of the best and brightest of our society who, when they had the choice, elected to work elsewhere. Not being able to attract these people has always been costly to the industrial institution, which supplies the nation's manufactured goods and has an extraordinary impact on the nation's standard of living.

Current history has led to an order–chaos dilemma. The past thirty years divide into three fairly distinct periods:

> (1) From 1965 to 1980, the U.S. suffered disastrous losses of market shares of manufactured goods, productivity gains were way below the pace of a hundred years, imports grew astronomically, exports stagnated, and we lost millions of high-paying jobs.

(2) In the 1980s, came the wakeup call, and industry was revitalized around AMTs, techniques such as TQM, JIT, and CIM. Managers became infatuated with Japanese factory management techniques and, aided by eager consultants, borrowed most of these AMTs from Japan. Productivity, quality, delivery cycles, and inventory turnover all improved. Production managers once again were considered important and credible in their firms, and management morale bloomed anew.

(3) But all has not been rosy. For in the last five years, despite all the improvements that came about in this industrial renaissance, U.S. industry has not regained lost market shares, imports are high in spite of a weak dollar which makes our goods cheaper abroad, and industrial managers report that they are in "competitive gridlock," that foreign competition has improved its performance as much or more as they have, and that their competitive position has worsened.

As a result, it is increasingly clear that copying competitors' AMTs and "benchmarking" to be as good as the best is not the way to win in today's ever intensifying global competition. Emulating one's competitors, usually two to five years later, does not regain market share. It is a formula for surviving, but not for winning. It is also clear that the "order" path is a weak management approach to making manufacturing a competitive weapon.

So industry has a dilemma. It is seen as new, but it is actually the same old tradeoff between order and chaos, now much more visible because the sheer excellence and rapacity of global industrial competition has made it undebatable that to survive and grow, industry must perform at levels undreamed of ten years ago. AMTs, the order, and command-and-control approach won't cut it. What is missing? Has adversity taught us anything?

Amidst adversity, in fact because of it, we have learned that too much order and top-down control sentences the factory to mediocre performance. This idea has been preached since the thirties but today's conditions have made some managements realize that success in manufacturing in the industrialized high-cost nations now requires the minds, released energies, and innovation of all employees. No longer can order be imposed nor all important decisions be made centrally.

As a result, many companies are risking some chaos in order to unleash the latent power of employees at every level. Success stories are emerging about participative decision-making, working with unions to settle policy decisions by consensus, problem-solving by teams, work organized by small groups instead of assembly lines, and endless, constant communication.

New human resource practices are also proving effective, especially pay systems based on learning additional skills, fewer and broader job classifications, non-supervised-self-led work groups, fewer supervisors with more employees, and broader flattened organizational structures. None of this works automatically, for it runs up against 150 years of industrial practice, and a mile or two of management bookshelves full of premises about the manager's requirement "to manage." Probably most important of all, these new practices require an unprecedented level of trust at all levels of management and at top levels an almost evangelical belief in the results which freedom and teamwork can produce.

Under the duress of unprecedented worldwide competition, we are learning that good management is not just order and control. Management that works in today's world is a mixture of order and enough freedom-based chaos to liberate eager spirits to innovate, develop their own methods and policies, and create competitive advantage from an explosion of pent-up energy.

What the factory seems to tell us about the human condition is that neither "pure chaos" nor "pure order" is very fruitful, not even survivable and certainly not sustainable. Pure chaos destroys any possibility of the powerful synergies latent in people working together. Pure order is stultifying to the spirit and arid in its ambiance. But the human being in the factory needs structure and, when given latitude to self-govern, happily creates a new order. Order is acceptable to the orderer but can be onerous to the ordered.

In the factory, perhaps as in life, individuals seek and cherish the value of clear, acceptable objectives. Those common purposes then provide a foundation of order which allows colleagues, released from work rules imposed from above, to work together untethered and energized to accomplish great and difficult things.

Wickham Skinner is James E. Robison Professor of Business Administration, Emeritus, Harvard University, and artist of the illustration for this essay.

EUGENE HOLLAHAN

The Decoy Carver

♦

S<small>CRIMSHAW WHALERS</small> and paddlewheel blues men,
watery makers, knew where they stood.
My skullduggery, no less native to these shores,

works on the marges between land and lake.
I learned on the Chesapeake how to mimic
the oily glide of mallard and canvasback.

No rest for my lures unless fowl take a dive.
Hollow at heart, I scoop out two halves of a tupelo.
Chiseling and crafty, with burrs and burning tools,

applying myself in the truest of false colors,
with many-colored coats I gloss the coot's glib self-deceit.
Nothing so reasonable as the treasonable.

Making themselves mere ducks and drakes,
gulling and pigeoning into my bucket shop,
heedless ringnecks put their heads in a noose.

Imagine my four-flushers adrift on a marsh,
shady and fishy, such stuff as dreams or vagrant bubbles.
Flyway ducks have their allurements. They fall for me.

Eugene Hollahan is editor of *Studies in the Literary Imagination* and professor in the Department of English at Georgia State University, Atlanta. He is secretary/treasurer of CELJ (Council of Editors of Learned Journals).

J. S. LINTON

Interventions
Pages from a Journal

♦

Mark's Wedding

Mark was not sure he wanted to get married, and he did not want to propose to Eliza at Christmas. Mark decided that if he was going to propose at all it would be in February, but not Valentine's Day. Mark is headstrong and handsome, but he was facing two determined women, Eliza, the potential bride, and Eliza's mother. Eliza was distraught but sympathetic to Mark. Eliza's mother was beyond distress; she was in the throes of concern that if the wedding was to occur, it needed to be organized, and she was the one who was going to organize it.

Mark and Eliza went to Delaware to spend Christmas with Eliza's parents. When they returned to Massachusetts, they were engaged. Reason had prevailed. How exactly this had come about I do not know, and I didn't need to know. I am Mark's mother. I love him and liked Eliza, whom I have come to love. I appreciated the situation Carolyn, Eliza's mother, was in. One cannot linger indefinitely on the sidelines if a wedding is going to be held. Carolyn had waited patiently for months while Mark and Eliza sorted out their relationship. But time was going by, and the limbo Mark's obstinacy created could not continue indefinitely, especially for Carolyn, if she was expected to orchestrate the wedding.

The engagement ring was selected and the wedding date set. But this was only the beginning for Carolyn. Now she could act, she could choreograph the wedding, craft it, and locate it in beautiful surroundings.

Grosz, George. *Tangle of Lives*. Drawing, twentieth century. The Detroit Institute of Arts, Gift of Dr. and Mrs. Hanns Schaeffer.

A formal wedding must not allow for chaos. It is a ritual which is given a specific time frame. The arrival of the guests, the appearance of the groom, his best man, and the minister, the procession of the ushers and the bridesmaids, the entrance of the bride and whomever is giving her away, the actual ceremony, the exchange of rings, the moment of transformation in the lives of the marrying couple, all of this requires deliberate and acute attention.

So Carolyn put the wedding into order. The wedding dress, the bridesmaids' dresses, the seating of guests, the arrangements of flowers, the order of the receiving line, the large tent for the reception and the dance floor beneath it, the tables set up for supper, the foods, the wedding cake, the musicians, the photographers, and the calculation of time for the photographs. Everything, everything had to be held in mind. For weeks before the wedding Carolyn covered sheets of paper with lists. The day of the wedding these lists were in Carolyn's pocketbook and in the hands of her friends she had selected to help her. It was a tremendous task, one in which there could be no mistakes.

And there were none. The summer wedding day was beautiful, the guests looked their best, the wedding party was elegantly attired, the bride was lovely, the groom was handsome and self-assured, and the ceremony was properly stylized and properly moving.

Only one unspecified event occurred. After the marriage ceremony concluded and before the bride and groom walked down the aisle, the bride spontaneously embraced and kissed her husband. It happened so quickly; it was the quintessence of loving expression. It was a gesture that caught the witnesses unaware and rendered them silent. It was the moment of the marriage when the transcendent level of this beautiful event was made manifest.

◆

Footsteps

I WAS SITTING IN THE LIVING ROOM of our home in Newark, Delaware. I was seven years old, home alone from school that afternoon because I had a cold. My father was at work, and my mother had left the modest house we were renting. She had gone out to accomplish errands, although it was raining steadily. It was an autumn rain, the sort that takes the lingering leaves from the trees. I sat in the living room, watching the rain through the window as the soaking brown leaves of the young oak tree in our front yard detached from their branches and slowly turned toward the lawn. There was no noise, and I was motionless, held in an atmosphere of aloneness.

The second floor of our house was quiet too, except for the gentle tap made by the occasional leaf brushing the window pane as it dropped to the ground. On the second floor was a corridor which ran between my parents' bedrooms; my father's room at one end and my mother's room at the opposite. My own little room was between these at the top of the staircase, next to which was the bathroom. There was nothing else on the second floor with the exception of an unfinished large closet off my father's room which was used as storage.

Suddenly I heard a noise upstairs in the hallway at my father's door. My attention was immediately riveted to this noise. There was no further sound, and my body relaxed a bit. Until then I had not realized I had tensed every muscle in my body. I told myself the noise was simply a matter of "the house settling," an expression I had heard but never witnessed. But within a minute the noise occurred again. This time there was no question in my mind that I was hearing footsteps. Slow footsteps, going from my father's doorway down the hall. I was riveted to my chair and breathless. I questioned who could possibly be upstairs. Reason told me no one could be there. When my mother left me to do her errands, we had both been upstairs talking as she prepared to leave. We hadn't gone into my father's room, but then, there was no need to do so. When she was ready to leave, we had both gone downstairs. I saw her to the front door, waved goodbye, and closed the door. I picked up the Nancy Drew mystery I was reading and sat on the footstool in front of my father's easy chair. But, now setting the book down, I concentrated on the footsteps.

The noise of the walking was sure, steady, and unhurried,

moving past the door to my room and along the corridor to my mother's bedroom door. There was a pause; then the steps turned and proceeded back along the hallway to my father's room. After a slight pause, the steps turned again and proceeded to my mother's doorway. Unlike the first visit to my mother's door entrance, the steps proceeded into the room. Then there was no more sound.

The fine hairs on the back of my neck rose. I was transfixed, but there was an imperative command within me that ordered me to go upstairs. Our staircase was arranged in such a way that one climbed three steps to a landing, then the steps turned ninety degrees and proceeded up several more stairs to a second landing where they again made another ninety-degree turn. From the second landing it was possible for me to see the ceiling of my bedroom. I paused; the house was absolutely still. My position was untenable, and I forced myself to climb the remaining steps to the hall.

I crept along the hall toward my mother's room. When I reached the threshold, I paused. Everything looked as it had, the furniture was all in order, and the dressing table was as my mother had left it. No one was there! And then I saw it. My mother had a comforter on her bed. It was soft, plush, and covered in a dark purple fabric, perhaps satin. I stared at the comforter in amazement, for on it was the impression of a body.

I turned and quietly went down the hall to the stairs. I descended noiselessly and returned to the footstool in the living room.

The afternoon was darkening. I sat, almost not daring to breathe. In time my mother returned, and then my father came home from work. I was so relieved by their presence, but I never told either of them of the footsteps or the form.

♦

Arnie

THE STUDENTS CAME INTO THE CLASSROOM as students usually do, in small groups, sidling in as though they were self-assured, but, because they had never been in this particular class before, they were uncertain, and whether realizing it or not, they slid as unobtrusively as possible into their seats. The difference between these scholars and undergraduates was that these people were Elderhostelers over sixty who would be together only one week. Elderhostel students come to learning sites situated all over the country for a variety of reasons. They may come because a site is in a region never been to before, because it is near relatives they wish to visit, or because they are genuinely interested in one of the three courses being given that week. As an Elderhostel teacher, it is interesting to determine just why a student is in one's class.

The class I was teaching during one lovely fall week in Connecticut was "Insights of Joseph Campbell." To begin, I introduced myself, spoke of my background as a teacher, and gave some introductory remarks about Campbell. We were well enough into the material that I could already discern that the class in general was interested in Campbell, if not captivated. Suddenly one of the students jumped out of his chair, waved his arms, and demanded to know why the class should be learning about Joseph Campbell, a mythologist, of all things, an American mythologer who came from a wealthy family. This accusation was untrue. Campbell's family was of moderate means. His access to time, or lack of work, was provided by the Great Depression, and he lived in the family summer home on almost nonexistent means. There was a pause after the student's outburst during which I rallied my justifications for teaching Campbell and let the class relax into my aura of competence. After some soothing words, my irate student sat down.

The next part of the class was a short video of Campbell's life. Some of the scenes showed Joseph on skis in Switzerland, in a bookstore in Paris, and on a ship getting up from a dining table to dance with an attractive young woman. The tape went on to reveal Joseph in the family summer cottage, surrounded by books. The narrator described the many, many months Joseph spent reading world mythology. While the tape was playing, I studied my class list and determined that my disgruntled student's name was Arnie; his wife's name was Imelda. The video concluded and after a few more words, I dismissed the class. Arnie left grumbling audibly.

Elderhostels are set up so that the students live in a dormitory, take their meals together, and can participate in activities planned for their free time. By the end of the first full day, the students have only begun to know each other, but certainly everyone knew Arnie, and everyone knew he thought Joseph Campbell an effete dilettante in an obscure subject.

And so Day Two began. My class was warmer, friendlier, and more voluble, including Arnie. During class, he voiced his objections to Joseph Campbell. He loudly restated that Campbell came from a wealthy family and had the time to "fool around with mythology," a subject both "useless and irrational." The class began to grumble against Arnie's interruptions, but Arnie complained on. Some class members became increasingly voluble refuting Arnie. Anarchy was ascending. By the conclusion of that second class we were in turmoil. I needed to turn the disagreements around between Arnie and his classmates before my subject and my teaching were lost beneath an avalanche of ill will. It was evident that Campbell and a harmonious atmosphere of shared learning were in jeopardy.

While the Elderhostlers were milling about before lunch, I searched for Arnie. When he saw me approach, he gave me a somewhat sidelong look and an inconclusive grin. I went up to him and said, "Arnie, I am so glad you are in my class." He gave an incredulous stare. I continued, "You are an immense value to the class because . . ."

"Stop. Wait." he said quickly. "Immie has got to hear this!" and he wheeled away from me, searching for Imelda. He quickly returned with his wife saying to me, "Tell her." I repeated what I'd said and continued.

"Arnie, if it weren't for you, the class would not be so dynamically interested in Joseph Campbell. But with you in class, the students have to think about Campbell, what he studied, what he wrote about, and what the components of his conclusions were."

"Did you hear that? Did you hear that?" he demanded of Imelda.

I immediately guessed Imelda had been taking him to task for his interruptions during class.

The doors to the cafeteria opened. The group filed in, filed through the lunch line, and seated themselves at various tables. But not Arnie. He beamed as he table-hopped, telling everyone how much he was contributing to our class. He said I said so. He said, "ask her," meaning me, "she'll tell you." His genial spirits rose and soared. It was as though a sun had come into his personality.

The next day, during class, the group was truly with me. They listened, laughed, asked questions, and, when Arnie became too vocal, too time consuming, they told him to be quiet, and he in all good grace, stopped talking, temporarily. The week became vitalizing. The students became happily friendly with each other and with me. As for Arnie, we all learned to keep him in line. He himself learned to keep within the bounds of decorum. We ended the week in a spirit of order and joy.

Jennifer S. Linton received her doctorate in English at Tufts University. She also holds a master's degree in art from Vanderbilt University.

◆ *GREGORY L. BAKER* ◆

Motion: A Spectrum of Order

◆

WE HAVE AN INNATE SENSE that the physical world is ordered. Even as young toddlers, taking our first steps, we trusted that the ground was immovable, and our developing muscles gradually adapted to the constant effect of gravity. Our movements evolved from careful experimentation to automatic gracefulness as we developed confidence in the permanence of our environment.

Permanence is a prerequisite for the discovery of order. Without permanence there is no pattern, predictability, or even trustworthy characterization of our physical surroundings. Yet our world is filled with motion and variety, resulting from the dynamics of interacting forces. That fundamental permanence resides in the *law-like* behavior of nature and in physical constants that can be expressed and measured as mathematical formulas and laws. Newton's laws of motion and gravity, for example, seem to describe fairly accurately the permanence of the cycles of planetary motion in our solar system.

It is remarkable that we can recreate in the laboratory a variety of motions and patterns found in our everyday surroundings. *But even more remarkable* is the fact that such motions appear as both *ordered* and *random*. One of science's mysteries is how the *law-like* behavior that we associate with order may contain within it the seeds of randomness—the very antithesis of order.

Let us begin with one of the best known laws of physical science:

$$Force = Mass \times Acceleration$$

Lautermilch, Steven. *Labyrinth*. Photograph.

This statement is Isaac Newton's second law of motion, first published in his *Principia* in 1687.[1] One typical example of this law is the motion of the driven pendulum. We may think of the motion of a child on a swing as a realistic approximation to the pendulum's motion. In this case, Newton's law can be particularized as follows:

> Mass (of the swing plus child) × its Acceleration =
> (1) the downward force of gravity
> + (2) the inhibiting force of friction
> + (3) the periodic forcing caused by the pusher

Gravity pulls the pendulum to the vertical position, but the pendulum's own inertia helps the motion to continue past the lowest point. Friction causes the pendulum to lose energy leading to a gradual decay of the motion, but periodic forcing infuses the system with energy, revitalizing all the various motions. Beginning with the example of a child on a swing, we can show mathematically how the motion of a pendulum can be measured as relatively constant or regular, as chaotic, and as semi-random.[2]

The Dynamics of Three Types of Motion
Regular Motion

EXPERIENCE WITH PUSHING A CHILD ON A SWING tells us that the child will get a pleasant back-and-forth motion if we push the swing

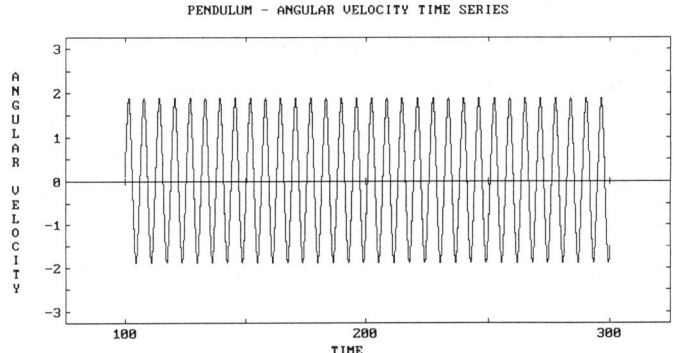

Figure 1. A graph of the pendulum's velocity over time, generated by a computer through appropriate manipulation of the mathematical equation, shows that the motion is completely regular and predictable. The pendulum is pushed at its natural frequency as one would push a child's swing.

at just the right frequency. Any initial bumpiness will disappear, and the swing will move in a *periodic, regular* manner. The frequency of push for this smooth motion is called the *resonant* frequency, and it depends primarily on the length of the swing and the strength of the earth's gravitational field. Because the motion is periodic, the swing's velocity goes from zero at the extreme displacement to a maximum as the swing passes through the lowest point, to zero at the other extreme, and then through a (negative) maximum as it passes through the lowest point traveling in the opposite direction as it moves toward an extreme point again. This cycle is repeated as long as the pusher applies the appropriate periodic forcing.

This motion can be represented as a *time series*, a series of values of the pendulum's velocity at closely spaced points in time (Figure 1). The regularity and periodicity of the motion is obvious. Clearly the motion is *ordered*.

Chaotic Motion

CHAOTIC MOTION ARISES when the pendulum is strongly pushed at a frequency that is *not* the resonant frequency. There is a competition between the restoring force of gravity (manifested through the resonant frequency) and the pushing at the non-resonant frequency. This competition leads to the unstable

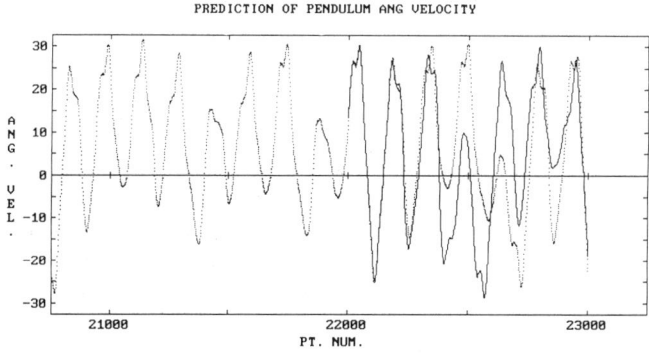

Figure 2. A graph of the pendulum's velocity over time.
The pendulum is strongly forced at two-thirds of the natural frequency.
The competition between the forcing and the pendulum's natural motion leads to unstable and chaotic behavior. Note that the motion never repeats exactly.

motion we call *deterministic chaos*. If it were implemented with a child's swing, this motion would result in a very uncomfortable ride. The motion never entirely repeats itself, and the child's sense of permanence felt through periodic motion would completely disappear. Furthermore, because the motion is always changing, the state of the system is affected by how it was started. In fact, if another identical swing were started with very slightly different conditions, its motion would eventually become completely different from that of the original swing. The system never "settles down" and, as a result, it is unpredictable over long times. Fortunately, such unsettling motion would be very difficult to achieve on a child's swing for any length of time with only human pushing. But these characteristics have been reproduced in mechanical pendula and a variety of other systems and many everyday examples, including meteorological phenomena. Chaos is ubiquitous!

A time series for a chaotic motion is represented in Figure 2. The forcing frequency is two-thirds of its resonant frequency, and its strength is about twice that of the previous case. While there is still a very strong component of the motion at this new forcing frequency, there is also a great deal of irregularity. It is remarkable that even with precise values for the forcing strength and frequency, the motion is highly irregular. The motion is deterministic—

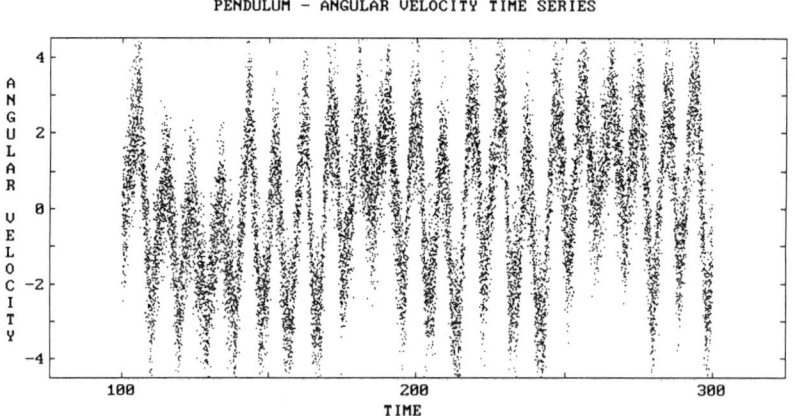

Figure 3. A graph of the velocity of a chaotic pendulum with a small random perturbation added to the velocity.

because it follows a deterministic law—but chaotic. Any order that resides in chaotic systems is subtle and obviously less tangible than in regular systems.

Semi-Random Motion

IN THIS LAST CASE we add a little randomness to the motion of our previously chaotic pendulum. One might imagine that the exertions of the pusher of the swing are slightly erratic so that we have perturbed a chaotic pendulum with random disturbances that we might think of as a kind of static or experimental error, called *noise* (Figure 3). The time series for velocity now has some aspects of deterministic chaos and some aspects of randomness. (The added "noise" is *not* represented in our mathematical equation. It is an addition that is produced by some small changes in the computer simulation of the equation.)

The Geometry and the Strange Attractors

MATHEMATICIANS AND PHYSICISTS use *geometry* to help them visualize the workings of their equations. In a conventional three-dimensional geometry we place points according to spatial positions. Using a *phase space* which is three-dimensional, a choice which is easy to depict on paper (Figures 4, 5, and 6), we will use *delay coordinates* for the three directions. These are the pendulum's velocity ω(t) at a time *(t)* [as one direction], its velocity at a somewhat later time *(t+T)* [as the second direction], and its velocity at a still later time *(t+2T)* [as the third direction]. For example, one point in the phase space might be positioned using velocity values at the times, 345, 348, and 351 so that $t = 345$ and $T = 3$.

Figure 4 shows a *phase portrait* for **regular motion**. In time, the system (represented by the delay coordinates) travels around a closed, periodic orbit. The periodic orbit correlates well with the

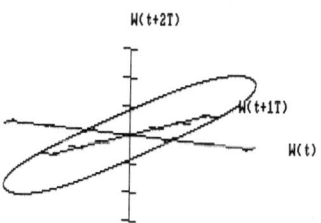

Figure 4. The phase space portrait of the regular motion originally depicted in Figure 1. The motion is described by a point that periodically traverses the closed loop. This structure is called an *attractor* and is one-dimensional— as is any line or curve.

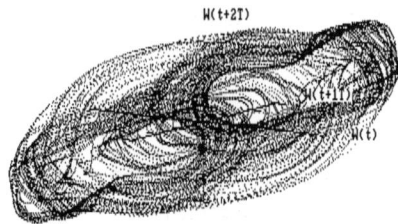

Figure 5. The phase portrait of the chaotic motion from Figure 2. The chaotic motion is represented by a point which travels around the *strange attractor* (of dimensionality 2.4).

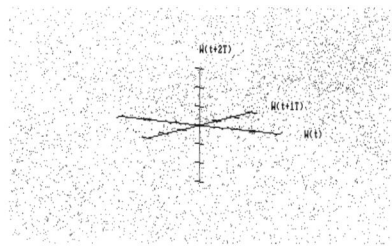

Figure 6. The phase portrait of the semi-random motion. The attractor now loses all structure and its dimensionality is never well-defined. As represented by this phase portrait, order in the motion seems to have disappeared.

periodic nature of the time series in Figure 1. This curve in phase space is called the *attractor* of the motion since all initial states of the pendulum give rise to motions that lead to this geometry.

Figure 5 is the corresponding phase portrait for **chaotic motion** (Figure 2). Now the system follows a path which never closes, never returns to the same state. This results in a structure that *partially fills* the space. In fact, if there were an infinite number of points in the time series, the phase space structure would consist of infinite layerings with infinite numbers of infinitely small spaces between them. This attractor is a strange kind of geometry called a *fractal* and is, in some sense, more than a two-dimensional surface but less than a three-dimensional volume. This fractal, therefore, has a non-integer dimensionality that is calculated to be about 2.4. Because of its fractal nature, this attractor is called a *strange attractor*. We see that the differences between regular and chaotic motion are dramatic in the phase space representation.

Figure 6 is the phase portrait of the **semi-random** time series (Figure 3). Once again the geometry changes dramatically with the addition of new complexity from random fluctuations added to the chaotic motion. Now the phase structure is completely space-filling. Unlike the previous attractors which have well defined dimensionalities (1 and 2.4), this geometry will expand to fill phase spaces of higher dimensionality than the three dimensions used in these diagrams. There is *no* defined value for the dimensionality of the phase portrait. This property is characteristic of random motion.

Phase space geometry dramatically portrays major distinctions between the three types of motion. Regular motion produces a one-dimensional periodic structure; chaotic motion gives rise to a 2.4-dimensional infinitely layered fractal; and semi-random motion produces a space-filling set of points of undefined dimension.

Prediction

A FUNDAMENTAL GOAL OF SCIENCE is to achieve sufficient understanding of a given phenomenon to forecast its future. For our three motions, the level of prediction is correspondingly varied. Figures 1 and 4 show that a forecast of the future for regular motion simply requires repetition of the past. The periodic behavior will continue indefinitely; and, therefore, the prediction time is infinite.

For chaotic motion the story is very different: prediction is possible, *but* only for a short time. The fundamental limitation is the sensitivity of the system to small changes in state. Figure 7 shows the time series for an experimental chaotic pendulum. At the data point numbered 22000 a prediction mechanism is invoked whose algorithm uses only earlier data. The prediction (the solid line) may

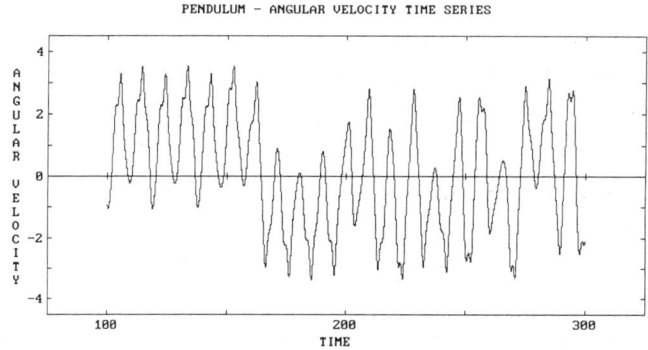

Figure 7. Forecast of data from an experimental chaotic pendulum.
The solid line is the prediction from the prior time data whereas the dotted line is real data that continued to be observed after the prediction began.
Obviously, the validity of the prediction is short-lived.

then be compared with the "real" future of the time series as shown by the dotted line. It is clear that this prediction (like a weather forecast) is only valid for a limited time, yet another major distinction between regular and chaotic motion.

Finally, consider the prediction time of the semi-random system. Application of the same methods used for the chaotic system show that the semi-random system is mostly unpredictable.[3] Since the future is completely uncertain, we conclude that the random perturbations on the pendulum's velocity destroyed whatever predictability there was in the chaotic pendulum. In this context the semi-random system is disordered.

Are there conclusions one can draw about the *order* inherent in these three types of motion? First, we note that regular motion is the most ordered in the obvious ways. It has the most easily defined appearance both in the real space where we usually view its motion as well as in the phase space with its periodic attractor. Furthermore it is predictable for arbitrarily long times into the future. Chaotic motion appears to be less ordered. Its time series never quite repeats previous behavior, the attractor is complex, and the prediction time is finite. On the other hand, there is a *richness* of behavior in chaotic motion that is unavailable to periodic motion. Its attractor occupies more dimensions of phase space—there is discretely more complexity and more *interest* in the appearance of the strange attractor. There is increasing evidence that this richness provides a mechanism for complex biological systems.[4] Both types of motion are governed by Newton's deterministic law of motion and, in some sense, both take their *order* from the order inherent in that law. The difference is that regular periodic motion is stable while chaotic motion is unstable. Finally, we note that the addition of random noise to the chaotic motion seems to drastically reduce the amount of order—the attractor is undefined and the prediction time becomes short.

Let us go a step further with our threefold characterization of motion in terms of dynamics, geometry, and prediction. Suppose that we draw some parallels—admittedly speculative—with the structure used by Swedenborg to describe various aspects of God and humans; namely, essence, form or manifesting, and proceeding. When describing the trinity, for example, Swedenborg writes:

> This trine is being (esse) manifesting (existere) and proceeding (procedure) for being must be manifested, and, when it is manifested, it must proceed that it may produce.

He then goes on to illustrate this with an angel (and presumably all humans) as follows:

> the being of an angel is what is called his soul, his manifesting is what is called his body, and the proceeding from both is what is called the sphere of his life, without which an angel has neither existence nor being.[5]

In our discussion of motion and order, we suggest that the thing itself, its being or essence, is the dynamics of the system as seen in its physical motion and the related time series. Next the phase space geometry provides a form or manifestation which graphically highlights differences in order between the various motions. And finally, prediction plays the role of that which goes forth (proceeds) from our understanding of the system. (In fact, for the chaotic system, both the dynamics and phase space geometry—a marriage of substance and form—are necessary to implement the prediction process.) While the analogy may not be perfect, it is compelling enough to remind us of the generality of the Swedenborgian trinal construct. The properties of the various motions and the suggested parallelism are collected in the table below.

The concept of order in the motions of physical systems is subtle. We have shown a spectrum of apparent order in different types of motion with regular motion as the most ordered and

	Regular	Chaotic	Semi-random	
Dynamics	Periodic Stable Deterministic	Never repeats Unstable Deterministic	Erratic Unstable Random perturbations	Essence
Geometry	Attractor Periodic orbit Dimension = 1	Strange attractor Infinitely many unstable orbits Dimension = 2.4	No attractor Random scatter Dimension undefined	Form (Manifest)
Prediction	Prediction time is infinite.	Prediction time is short.	Prediction time is about zero.	Proceeding

random motion as the most disordered. Yet even our short discussion suggests that chaotic systems display a richness of behavior not found in regular motion. Does this richness imply greater complexity and consequently greater order? Are chaotic systems really more ordered than regular systems? As this twentieth century draws to a close we are reminded that physical science of the late nineteenth century seemed on the verge of a comprehensive understanding of nature. Yet revolutionary scientific events of the early twentieth century showed that vision to be a mirage. While our understanding has increased vastly so also has our ignorance. Scientists can reasonably and eagerly anticipate that the twenty-first century will bring new insights and new questions to many old problems, including the much-discussed concept of order.

Gregory L. Baker is professor of physics at the Bryn Athyn Academy. He received his doctorate from the University of Toronto for his work in nuclear quadrupole resonance spectroscopy and has been published in numerous journals. He is co-author, with Jerry Gollub, of *Chaotic Dynamics: An Introduction* (Cambridge University Press), and author of *Religion and Science: From Swedenborg to Chaotic Dynamics* (Solomon Press, New York).

Notes

1. Newton, I. A. Motte, trans., 1729; final ed. revised by A. Cajori. *Sir Isaac Newton's Mathematical Principles of Natural Philosophy.* Berkeley: California Press, 1934. First published in Latin as *Philosophiae naturalis principia mathematica*. London: Streater, 1687.
2. For a more comprehensive treatment of the driven pendulum as a chaotic system, see Baker, G. L. and J. P. Gollub, *Chaotic Dynamics: An Introduction*. Cambridge University Press, 1990. For a general treatment of chaotic dynamics at a non-mathematical level, see Gleick, J., *Chaos: Making of a New Science.* New York: Viking, 1987.
3. Methods do exist for recovering some information from noisy systems; therefore, some prediction is still possible if the system is fundamentally deterministic.
4. L. A. Lipsitz and A. L. Goldberger. Loss of "complexity" and aging: Potential applications of fractals and chaos theory to senescence. *Journal of the American Medical Association* 267 (1992): 1806–1809.
5. Swedenborg, E. *Apocalypse Explained* (first published in Latin, Stockholm, 1759). J. Whitehead, trans. New York: Swedenborg Foundation, 1911. Paragraph 1111.

SUSAN FLAGG POOLE

The River

♦

One grain of sand,
one thoughtless word too many,
and the balance tilts.
Sand moves ever so slightly.
Trickles turn, slopes shift,
and the dune collapses.

A breath of wind in a coral sky
reforms the surface
while a beetle climbs the avalanche.
An underground river
snakes across the desert,
carrying everything with it.

Susan Flagg Poole completed her master's degree in educational psychology. An educator, writer, and mother, Susan is a sixth-generation Swedenborgian.

WALTER R. CHRISTIE

A Brief Moment of Confusion about the Nature of God

♦

WHEN I WAS TWENTY, illuminated by the long light of an Alaskan summer, I stood in the tundra plain that drains Denali's glaciers and witnessed nature turned upside down. As the shadow of the moon eclipsed the sun's face, startled owls wheeled from nests, caribou stampeded, and mother grizzlies with cubs in tow bounded up hillsides in search of a safety that could not be found. In this wrent in nature's web, I saw connectedness of all being and was visited by a deeper identity that urged me to become a physician. Ever since, I have loved the alpine zone.

Given this deep love of the Arctic, it is strange that at fifty years of age, weary of the societal aspects of my professional life and needing another pilgrimage, I chose the steamy, equatorial island of Bali, where I would find no coolness, clarity, or integration but instead would risk torpor, disintegration, and a brief moment of confusion about the nature of God.

The choice of Bali grew from my attraction to the Divine Feminine, for although a psychiatrist by vocation, I am a romantic by nature and thus in love with a dream behind the world as well as its daily vicissitudes. In my long hours in public psychiatry working with the disintegrating energies of mental illness, I developed a deep longing for coherence of soul that promised to be met by the perennial philosophy of the Vedas and the rich symbolism of the Hindu pantheon, particularly the representations of the Mother Goddess. Expressed in me through love of marriage, home, and family, nature and gardening, the ocean and small boats, and

---

Naga, genius of the Nether World, detail. tenth century. In *Ideas and Images in World Art*, Rene Huyghe. New York: Harry N. Abrams, Inc.,1959. p. 27.

art, the Mother Goddess shaped the content and contemplative intent of my meditations, and, as psychiatry exhausted my reserves, this love turned me toward the Beloved Other and Paradise.

In my home state of Maine my lack of anonymity and my medical privilege had reduced my social world to a web of entangled relationships that were far too special, rarefied, and unreal. I yearned for open, spontaneous, expressive community, and Bali was said to be a place where psyche and community were totally interpenetrated, where all dimensions of the human soul were given room for expression within a balanced cultural order.

Maybe you've seen the ads for Bali—beautiful, exotic, childlike people in a temple dotted landscape that is both earthy and transcendent due to perfect balance of culture and nature. What better place for an alienated psychiatrist to find again that renewing seam of black soil at the core of his overcivilized soul?

Of course, the allure of Asia was part of it, too. Five years before, on the high plateau of Tibet, my beautiful and remarkable wife Elle experienced an ultimate solitude that bonded her forever to the Tibetan people. Now she hoped that as a couple we might have a journey as transformative as hers, and her love of the East had worked on me and induced my evolution from an unfocused neoJungian gnosticism toward a bhakti path of devotion to the actively cohering natural order and processes symbolized by the Mother Goddess.

Then in 1992–1993 I chanced upon documentaries on Bali that described a tropical, paradisiacal landscape shot through with animistic powers and yet simultaneously blessed with a highly developed Hindu ceremonial culture that perpetually recreated its relationship with the Divine through a profusion of crafts, painting, and the dance. Bali was also alleged to be a peaceful society that honored children, women, and the environment, and, conveniently for a searcher like me, it lay halfway around the world from the rocky coast where I had spent most of my life.

Then, too, I will confess that my choice of Bali at age fifty grew from the fact that I'm a Westerner, and the East is shadow. In the affluent West we believe that pleasures of Paradise can be purchased at will. Credit cards in hand, we carve out wedges of time to enjoy the haunts of the Goddess, and because this time of ours is so precious, we want all of Her sensuousness, spirituality, beauty, and fantasy—instantly—or we'll write Her off our list of planetary glamours. In this sense, then, I took a three-week leave from work in early summer 1993. The place I put down my money to encounter the Goddess was Bali, jewel of the Indonesia archipelago, The Morning of the World.

Of Bali too much and too little has been said. Too much has been said of the Western dream of tropical beaches, child-faced women with supple bodies, tiered rice paddies rising into the clouds, Hindu ceremonies fragrant with blossoms and holy water, the formal beauty of dances, and everywhere, everywhere art. Too little has been said about the psychic horrors of animistic ancestor worship and the restriction and fear inherent in an over organized society further tyrannized by a totalitarian, cruel, corrupt government. In particular, too little has been said about the dangers to the Western psyche of a culture that is permeated with animistic forces and hidden cruelties, yet presents itself, gaily and with appeal, as entirely compatible with the sensibilities of the average traveler.

This is not to say that the Western images of Bali are not true, because in Bali everything is true (and false). For centuries Bali has been a theater culture, and illusions are its daily business. Open and friendly, the Balinese often artfully allude to highly guarded community secrets, but without coaxing suddenly offer to share these precious initiations. Honored by such a secret, the traveler easily believes he or she has been drawn safely within a protective circle, but this casual unmasking is just part of the passing phantasmagoria. The real Bali is best known in the demon-dark hours before dawn when dogs howl, roosters crow, and presences drift across the smoky landscape.

My brief moment of confusion about the nature of God occurred before the main alter at Besakih, the Mother Temple, high on the slopes of Gunung Agung, the sacred volcano whose smoke mingles with clouds nearly two miles above the ocean. To understand the significance of this moment, however, let me briefly describe the terrain—geographically and psychologically—in the days before we came to Besakih.

Our group, by arrangement, was staying at a Gandhi ashram in the coastal town of Candi Dasa. The ashram-school complex, a former estate, was a core cluster of pavilions with a string of huts running along a sand spit, defined on the south by the churning waves of the Indian Ocean and on the north by a weedy lagoon whose waters upswelled near the base of a dragon toothed mountain just across the road. This volcanic spur was one of a string of lava plugs extending inland toward the huge cinder cones that formed Bali's central spine.

The director of the ashram, a Balinese woman of considerable personal and political power, not only took in guests to support the young Balinese who studied there, but she also arranged cultural trips to nearby sites and lectures on Gandhi beliefs, Hindu culture, and Balinese art. Her intent for our time in Bali was to organize completely the nature and quality of our experience. Protecting us, she did not relish outside influences. It was ironic, therefore, that the only person we knew in all of Southeast Asia was a friend formerly from our region of Maine, and quite synchronously she lived in Candi Dasa. The die was cast for our troubles.

In, preparing for the trip we looked forward to our friend's insider's view of the culture, but, as we met on our third night in Bali, we were saddened to discover that she was moving soon to Java. The reason, she explained, was that Bali was no longer healthy or safe for single Western women due to the unremitting sexual predation of Balinese men on women they perceived as moneyed. Culturally and economically suppressed, these bored and restless men courted the fantasies and sexual appetites of women travelers and the few unattached women who chose to live there. In the tragic wake of such predation our friend had seen her friends descend into promiscuity and addictions or leave the island. To her, leaving seemed the healthiest option.

Deeply disturbed by our conversation, Elle and I said good night and began our walk back through the warm, smoke scented darkness of Candi Dasa. Arm and arm as husband and wife, we were shocked when man after man appeared from the darkness to brush by Elle and murmur sexual offerings. I seemed to not exist for these men, and thus the seduction was doubly painful—violation for Elle and nonbeing for me. As a novice on the bhakti path of devotion to the Divine Feminine, I found the earthly woman I love in constant danger of exploitation, and there seemed little I could do to protect her from these mercenary overtures, for the shadows were filled with low buzzing conversations of faceless, squatting men.

In Bali economic predation is just business as usual as street vendors stream from everywhere and press you to buy art, art, art until you can look at no more art. It was the sexual commerce, however, that wore at our spirit, and no sidewalk, restaurant, or temple courtyard seemed free of these darker deals. I, too, was approached with offers and discovered that I could buy anything I wanted—any sex, age, combination.

Earlier in my life I might have been titillated, but each encounter was a horror, because its intent was so transparently about something other than the erotic allure it offered. Most importantly, what lay beneath these offers felt old and karmic—a carnal fire ignited by many brutal wars and exploitation of peoples and now fanned by a recessed economy and the nightmarish sex tourism of both West and East in a postwar petroleum rich, spiritually bankrupt world.

For reasons I cannot totally explain, as a representative of a high consumption, affluent society, I felt forced to endure the magnetizing darkness of these encounters. Although the content of the seductions had been scripted by those who came before me, I could find no way to escape them. Guilty by association, I was the affluent, powerful West in search of the Great Whore of the East, and no efforts at disavowal would release me from the relentless karma of this role.

Perhaps if the trip had not meant so much at a soul level to Elle and me, we might have dismissed the constant approaches just as city dwellers disregard honking cabs and panhandlers, but this particular form of cultural deterioration was tragically poised against the very reason we had come, namely to experience cultural beauty and spirituality in the context of the unviolated Feminine.

Compounding our isolation, members of the ashram and many of our fellow travelers offered little validation for our description of the blatancy of the predation. Like victims who must bear blame for their fate, we were reminded that we always could just say 'no' and walk away. As a result of these disqualifying messages, Elle and I increasingly withdrew from our hosts and traveling companions, and I stopped sleeping.

I did not lose sleep completely, but strong dreams woke me long before dawn. The dreams were weary, tattered images of women in danger with myself in the role of protector. As a dynamically trained psychiatrist I knew, of course, that such elements of dreams might be unacknowledged parts of my self, but, even if that were true at some level, to fully introvert the interpretive frame seemed inappropriate in the presence of real evil.

As nights passed, and I grew more sleep deprived, I was gripped by a distinct, undeniable feeling that this place, despite its comforts, was inimical to my deeper self, that it would wear me down, and it might even destroy aspects of my being—forever. I considered the great possibility that my needs for intimacy and verbal-conceptual understanding made me a weak limb on the Balinese tree, and soon I would either break off in the storm of my own psychic life or be sawed off by some courteous, smiling Balinese gardener. As an experienced psychiatrist, I knew I was at risk of serious regression.

At this time Elle noted that the ocean seemed too loud. As enthusiastic denizens of the rocky coast of Maine, we are well used to sleeping in the roar of surf, but this constant thunder from the beach seemed unnatural.

Also at that time I noticed that the preferred religious life of the ashram did not seem to be the predawn chanting of the beautiful passages from the Vedas or the Socratic rendering of Gandhi's aphorisms at the director's highly controlled morning pujah, but instead took place in late afternoon ceremonies in the two-tiered temple across the road.

Coalescing into a still unnamable pattern, our observations convinced us that here much was wrong with the Feminine. Day by day we saw the limited, oppressed role of hardworking Balinese women while we continued to endure the predation of the bored, economically marginalized men (as well as the small boys who assisted them). Although ashram life was peaceful, and we were offered the best of Gandhi's nonviolent thinking, the teachings seemed dissociated from the place and suffered from a subtle violence, as if the director's concern that Balinese culture could not meet the challenges of the modern world had polarized the ashram against the ancient animistic, preliterate, magical culture it sought to transform.

Soon Elle's detective work revealed that Candi Dasa's ocean roared so loudly because a few years before developers had blown up the protective ocean reef to mine coral to build hotels and roads. We guessed that the ocean then rushed into the lagoon behind our cottage, and the lagoon had to be dammed to prevent salination, thus denying its usual free flow of water, eutrophying, and choking itself on a thick green mass of weeds.

At this point I desperately needed action to fend off further regression. As a nature oriented person, I had some skills in reading landscape, so I called upon both feng shui practitioner as well as the physician in me to diagnose our eco–psycho–spiritual problem. Deciding to use my sleepless hours productively, I crept out of the ashram long before anyone stirred for morning pujah and crossed the road to the two-tiered temple.

In the dim light of the starry heavens, I slipped into the sunken courtyard of the fertility goddess. Well placed in a pale stone grotto, the goddess, holding her many children, stared out with impassive but kind eyes toward those who came seeking her help. As I studied her rounded form, posture, and positioning in the stone, I felt a certain peacefulness, and the cool pre-dawn air contributed to the pleasure of this moment with her.

Taking leave of the goddess, I climbed the long narrow steps to Siwa's temple. The Lord of Creation and Destruction was worshipped in a fortress-like palisade of carved walls among the scrubby trees on a higher step of the dragon-tooth hill. Near the entrance a primal goddess stood with wide vulva and wild-eyed demons, swathed in checkered cloth, watching all directions and doorways. Siwa's draped phallus rose strange in the darkness, but the air was sweet with ashes of incense and pellucid remains of withering frangipani petals. Feeling peaceful, I leaned over the wall, gazed at the dark ocean, and waited for the dawn.

As the sun rose over Bali's central spine of volcanoes, light spilled down toward Candi Dasa, and I saw clearly the elements of the ocean, the mined reef, the sand spit and its ashram cottages, the algae clogged lagoon, the dragon-toothed hill, and the relationship of all to each other. Clearly the lagoon had been the upswelling womb of the Mother Goddess whose life-giving waters once flowed through Her sacred yoni to the sea.

Seeing all of this, I realized, painfully, that this place where Elle and I tried to sleep lay between two desecrated waters—indeed a double violation of the Feminine, and thus the effort to teach Gandhi's sacred nonviolent individuality seemed such sad business in a violated mythic landscape whose animistic energies, although weakened by the forces of progress, still prevailed in dissociated anger at what had been done to their matrix—the earth and the sea.

Partly relieved by my understanding, yet at another level even deeper in despair, I returned to the cottage to meditate until Elle awoke. I needed to cultivate energy, because this day we would go to Besakih, The Mother Temple of Hindu Bali. I had so looked forward to this visit to Besakih, because this was the place where I now, consciously, hoped to meet the Mother Goddess.

For over an hour our van wound its way up misty, jungled foothills, past tier after tier of cascading rice paddies, until suddenly the sharp pitch of the road told us we were ascending the sacred volcano. Above us, thick gray clouds obliterated the barren rim of Agung's crater and intermittently spattered warm rain over the jungle and the acres of temples that comprised Besakih—The Mother Temple whose invisible tethers floated seaward in all directions to bind each of Bali's major Hindu temples to the Sacred Mountain and the Center of the World.

Elle and I were so excited that not even the shopping center of craft shops by the parking lot, the crowds of tourists and Balinese devotees, or the corridor of vendors lining the long stairs upward could distract us from our intention to have, fate willing, a spiritual experience uncomplicated by animistic darkness or the soul wearying commercialism of Bali's tourist economy.

Wrapping our saris to be presentable, we began the slow climb past high tiered towers that were guarded by fearsome demons and graced with long arches of rice leaves flickering in the moist breeze. Still higher, the temple multiplied into many temples whose ornate details were almost too much to see and comprehend. Increasingly anxious with the visual overstimulation and the crowds surging behind me, I kept climbing and waiting for directions from our guides. The guides, both members of the ashram, were our driver and a young Balinese woman with considerable presence. He would negotiate permission for us to enter the inner sanctum of the central holiest alter, and she would bring offerings and speak with the women priests.

At the threshold of the sanctum Elle's mood seemed light. As she climbed the long flight of steps, she had been buoyed up by a powerful energy that seemed to issue from the core of the volcano, and this force lifted her up the hillside as if she were floating. The pure ease and the uniqueness of the experience fascinated her. I, on the other hand, had been anxious for the entire walk. Frustrated by so many disappointing elements of Bali, I really needed something to happen here.

The next moments are somewhat of blur. We were ushered through the gate, toward the main alter. Two women priests took our offerings and gestured for us to kneel. Smoldering incense sticks were driven into cracks in the stones before us, and we were instructed to bow our heads. Petal sweetened holy water splashed over our heads and down our cheeks. The women priests chanted, poured more holy water, and then with deft movements of their thumbs pressed clusters of rice grains to our wet foreheads.

Despair hollowed my belly, and blood drained from my face, for both this place and my inner world seem terribly flat and colorless. Beneath me, dark with holy water and stained with the ash of incense sticks, the paving stones seemed a sad, ugly gray. I knew ultimate disappointment was inevitable, and it was at this moment of despondency that I looked up and had a brief moment of confusion about the nature of God.

The moment was simple, shamefully simple. Looking up from the flat, gray, wet place where I had been kneeling to receive the holy water and rice, I saw before me looming behind the alter three gigantic monoliths, each swathed in a different color of cloth. A hot shock of recognition exploded in the empty place in my belly, and I knew immediately that here was the Triple Goddess. I had come to Besakih to meet the Mother, and in her innermost sanctuary I now met Her triple majesty. What a gift!

Dazed, I lingered on my knees while the rest of our party rose and shuffled toward the gate. Our guides were rushing us since there were many more pilgrims to kneel before the Mother this day. Aware of the others, but glad, exhausted, and embarrassed at my bewildered adoration I staggered to my feet and hurried after them. Our driver was standing by the arch to usher us through, and I was the last, so we walked together up the path that continued higher into the temple.

"The three stones," I stammered. "They were . . ." I hoped he would share my astonishment. He just nodded.

"Yes," he said calmly, "they are Brahma, Vishnu, and Siwa."

His words cut me like a knife. Instantly I knew he was right. How could I not recognize the omnipresent masculine representations of the Hindu triune God?

However, another voice in me said firmly, "No, you saw what you saw. That truly was the Goddess. This is Her temple. This volcano is Her. You saw past the cultural trappings to the Real. Do not let shame rob you of your vision!"

Worried that further conversation with the guide would leave me even more bereft, I pushed up the crowded path to find Elle.

"Did you see the Triple Goddess?" I asked. I wanted an answer, but I could see that she was in a spell.

"I've never felt anything like it," she stammered. "It was like I floated. My legs did no work."

I needed her to confirm for me that the Mother was here, and I wanted her confirmation to be passionate and certain.

"This is something, isn't it?" I said. I could feel the vision disqualifying shame returning.

"You needed to see the Goddess!" The hot voice of my shame erupted in my heart. "For that reason you saw Her. Walter, this is pure wish fulfillment at that. Even more tragically this is not very dramatic wish fulfillment at that."

"After all," the voice droned, "perceptually you saw exactly what the others saw. You were just too ignorant to name the stones correctly, so you made them what you wanted them to be. What a dreary piece of business—totally flat in imagination!"

"Wrong, wrong!" I protested, hoping the firm, believing voice would return to aid me. "I can't say why, but I know you are Wrong. Something did happen, something big."

"Big?" my shame scornfully replied. "No . . . very, very small—no auras, no visions, no radical intuitions, just the sad, painful wish of a tired man who needed something—anything—to ease his disappointment with the pilgrimage and himself."

At this point I saw the danger of this inner dialogue and stopped it. To further protect my fragile vision, I pushed past the others and climbed higher to a vista overlooking the vast jungle and the rice paddies that sloped toward the pale, flat Balinese sea.

This day in Maine, I thought, the late June sky might be high blue, and the ocean brisk with waves. The islands of Casco Bay might be dancing in the pure vibrancy of the waters, and if I were there—how I wish I were there—I would push the bow of our boat into the wind and enjoy every sparkle of wave and spatter of spray.

But I was here in torpid Bali where clouds hung like steam, and the sea seemed to be dying from lack of light. From my perspective high on the volcano the ocean clearly did look abysmal, just the way the Balinese describe it. Shame was reducing me. It was robbing my vision, and as it did, the landscape was claiming me. Deep inside, however, I knew that here at Besakih I had met the Mother Goddess No one could tell me otherwise.

It is one thing to have a vision, but another matter to keep it, so I closed my eyes and relived the moment at the alter to fix it in memory before the slow downward walk past clamoring vendors and swarms of tourists filming themselves with video cameras. I was very intent on keeping the presence of the Mother, but as I slipped past the distracting crowds, perspiration poured from my brow and loosened the rice pasted on my forehead. A few grains fell off and stuck to my eyebrows, making me feel even more awkward.

At the van I carefully removed my sari, folded it, and climbed into the seat next to Elle. The others were bartering with vendors while we sat quietly. Quiet, however, was not to be the nature of the rest of the day, for within less than an hour we were in the noisy markets of KlungKlung and touring the Hall of Justice with its beaming, toothy guide recounting disembowelments, castrations, and a variety of other sadistic punishments issued in medieval Bali for offenses such as lying or infidelity. Yet, as the guide leered and gesticulated at the gruesome images on the dome above us, I held my vision of the Mother dearly. In the uproar of the marketplace amidst slaughtered animal parts and the stink of public lavatories, I kept holding, holding my brief moment of confusion about the nature of God.

When we reached the Goa Lawah, however, The Bat Cave Temple by the abysmal sea, I could no longer fend off the eroding power of the profane. The temple's guano stained sanctum was a volcanic vent gaping open in the side of a ridge only a couple hundred yards from the bright beach itself. Hanging inside the cave's putrid maw, glossy black bats murmured of other realities while deeper within thousands of others fluttered through haunted vents that allegedly wound their way through lightless seams of volcanic stone all the way back to Besakih itself.

The extreme challenge to my vision of the Mother Goddess began with the onslaught of vendors who pressed around our van as it pulled into the parking lot. Waving saris and strings of wooden beads, they forced themselves upon us before we could exit the van, and, pushing strings of beads in our faces, they begged us to take them.

One young woman singled me out. I felt her do it. In her late twenties with brownish hair and somewhat Caucasian features, she gazed at me with a face resembling that of girls in my high-school class.

"I am San-dee," she said. "Take this necklace. It is a gift from San-dee."

I shrugged and gestured my lack of interest.

"Please," she said, "it is free. Take the necklace and come to my booth after you have visited the Temple. My name is San-dee. Come to my booth. I have art you can buy."

Hating my diffident role, I shrugged again and turned away.

"What is your name?" I shrugged again and pursed my lips.
"Walt," I said finally.

"Mr. Walt, my name is San-dee. Take my necklace as a gift and let me wrap your sari so you may go to the Bat Temple."

Deftly she looped the necklace around my neck and took the sari from my hand. Then she knelt in front of me, and with her face at my waist she gazed up and spoke slowly and with great intensity.

"Mr. Walt," she said, looking straight into my eyes. "You are very handsome, Mr. Walt. San-dee ties your sari for you."

Her light brown hair fluttered as she did her work, and every few seconds she looked up imploringly.

"Please come to my booth," she said.

In her eyes I saw past the erotic allure to a deeper desperation, to an impossible need, and in my role as the affluent West I felt again a deep compulsion to fulfill that need. Yet, this day I could not, for the cost to me was too high. My brief moment of confusion about God was at stake here, so I swallowed and let her finish swathing me in silk. Cinching the sari slowly at my waist and looking up at me with eyes as wide and hungry for light as the Balinese ocean, she spoke her command.

"Mr. Walt, come to my booth after you visit the temple. I have things that will please you. My name is San-dee.

What can I say? I did go to the temple as she directed, and I dutifully stared at the black opening and the piebald stains of bat guano dripping over the alter cloth, and then, feeling overwhelmed and emotionally numb, I turned to look at the Balinese sea. In Maine, I thought, the wind is blowing from the southeast, and spray is breaking over the stone jetty at the entrance of the harbor. Toward the outer islands flocks of eiders ride the swells while Black-backed Gulls call from the thermals above.

Her name is San-dee, I thought, and all I have to do to fulfill my appointed role is to go to her booth and make the purchase. If I do that simple act, then I can have my purchase, and I can have the fantasy of San-dee as she offered the beaded necklace, as she dropped to her knees with her face close to that part of me that would rise to meet her if we were lovers, as she told me how handsome I am, and as, with deft tugs of her probing fingers, she slowly tied the knot of my sari. All I have to do is go to her booth, make the purchase, and fulfill this role.

When I was boy in northern Maine, carnivals came to town in late summer or fall. They were fascinating spectacles of wild music, stomach-turning rides, and wonderful, bizarre freak shows. The people who came to enjoy them were amazing, too, for at no other time of year did I see so many tattoos and tight pants, stetsons and berets. When you're a kid, the things you dream about walk right up to you at a carnival.

Of course, there were forbidden things, too, like games of chance where bleached-blond women with husky voices like ancient sorceresses called the throws of dice and spin of wheels. Certainly, most forbidden of all was the strip show. Only grown men were allowed to go into that tent, but some of us boys slipped under the canvas and saw what the women did with their bodies and what the men did in return.

"Mister Walt, you are so handsome. My name is San-dee. Come to my booth. I have things that will please you."

Perhaps in my dotage I will think, why didn't I just make the purchase from San-dee and be done with it? Then I could have it all any way I wanted, both materially and imaginally, because that's what Bali is all about—having it any way you want it. My imagination, however, had become so weakened by alienation from my usual supports and by penetration of animistic forces that all I was capable of doing was holding onto what I absolutely needed for survival at the soul level. Thus, in its weakness my imagination had only enough energy for the sacred, because only the sacred would save me.

Slipping unnoticed past the vendor booths, I returned to the van and shut the doors. Elle was already inside. In the crowd I could see San-dee furtively searching for Mr. Walt. In seconds she was at my window.

"Mr. Walt. Please, Mr. Walt, you must come to my booth."

I could not listen to her without looking at her. I truly hated to deny her, so breathing deeply, I turned my face toward the glass.

"Mr. Walt," she was crying, "you must come to my booth."

Fine tears sparkled in the creases of her clenched eyes, and I knew, with sadness and shame, that they were born of stifled rage and helplessness. Besakih wavered in my mind, and around me a darkness began to descend.

I did not treat the darkness as real until we pulled out of the parking lot and were a short distance down the road. Light clouds floated over the ocean, and in the world of outer perception it was a beautiful day. By a white sand beach next to the highway a signpost had been driven into the sand. "Nude bathing prohibited," it said. Paradise ws closed for business. Reading the stark injunction, I felt the darkness descend.

The darkness is difficult to describe, because it was not real at the level of the senses, yet its reality was so sharp in my mind's eye that it superimposed itself on the world of light so that there was nowhere I could look in the brightness and color of this tropical island without experiencing the darkest of dark nights. Clinicians might be tempted to call this darkness a perceptual correlate of depression, but it was far more numinous than that, and with it came a flood of images that I would have never chosen to have.

The images began in south Bali on the tourist-jammed beach at Kuta, a place we did not visit on our journey. Boy and girl child prostitutes wandered the sands and mingled among the recliners where sunbathers, bodies slick with lotion and minds mellowed by cool beer, watched the seductive movements of the small bodies. In a hotel room just above the beach two Caucasian men and a Balinese woman, hazy with alcohol, snorted lines of white powder before falling upon each other in a chaos of lovemaking.

Then, instantly the darkness exploded, and its shock wave rippled across the vast vista of Asia and the Pacific. By the long sex warehouses of Bangkok, sailors' military whites floated ghostlike in a sea of dark vendors hawking clean, AIDS-free sex. In business offices of Tokyo, Manila, and Jakarta coiffured men in silk suits sipped drinks, puffed cigars, and set the prices for trade in arms, cocaine, heroin, virgin women, and unviolated children to feed the voraciousness of the postwar world.

Then, as if the darkness demanded that I see it all, the wave rolled eastward over the sprawling slum of cramped shacks on Saipan where Asian workers, lured by American textile firms with promises of the good life, sweltered their drab, joyous hours away. Then its crest kept running across miles of ocean toward the continental United States where a rusty steamer of uncertain port released human cargo from her stinking hold. Having paid dearly for their passage to freedom, the suffocating yellow-skinned people climbed clown a rotting rope ladder into a leaky wooden boat that would never see landfall.

This was the darkness that encircled San-dee and me, that encircled us all. We will never escape this, I thought. We have gone too far.

The darkness, however, was not done with me, for in its huge vibrating silence, trees crashed to the rainforest floor. Columns of fire shot skyward, and birds and monkeys screamed in terror as human-kindled firestorms raged through their leafy covers. Profit was everywhere; I could feel the banknotes in my fingers.

Filled with a sadness I cannot describe, I looked back toward the Bat Cave. If I asked, our driver would certainly turn around, and many in our party would applaud my decision to return and make the purchase from San-dee. Briefly, this idea seemed perfect, a just-right, concrete act to dispel the pain caused by the darkness. The full power of despair, however, suddenly welled in my chest. I did not dare speak, as any sound from my throat would reveal the presence of my disorder.

Back at the ashram, I once again tried to share my experiences with others, but they considered them all in my imagination. They were right, of course, but in a different way than they intended, so I finally heeded Elle's advice, stopped my search for empathy, and waited for the blessing of darkness when the world without would match my world within.

Each night in our cottage by the too-loud surf Elle and I lay sweating on narrow cots with posts at each corner like little four-poster beds. Heat forced us to sleep naked, and the white mosquito netting draped over these spindly posts created a gauzy world where we lay swaddled like infants and shrouded like corpses.

Miraculously I fell asleep only to be awakened about 10:30 PM by an wild scream that spun around and around the interior of the cottage. Astonished, Elle, too, bolted awake.

"What is it?" I gasped, as the sound whirled over me.

Before Elle could stammer an answer, the bed posts began to sway, and the shrouds over us fluttered and swished with the movement of the posts. The whirling sound grew maniacal, full of terror. The posts swung wildly, and the shrouds flounced an eerie white.

"It's an earthquake," I cried and fell back on the undulating bed.

Barely breathing, Elle and I lay rigid, while the sound whirled above us and then faded as the beds stopped their rocking movements.

"Walt?" Elle asked with a strange urgency. "Wasn't that the same sound you heard on the third night after your father's death?"

She was right. That was the sound that woke me from sleep on that third night after my father's aorta ruptured. At that strange moment years before, I had described to Elle the sound's strange qualities and the phenomena that accompanied it, but she had not actually heard it. Now without prompting she made the recognition.

The naturalistic explanation of the sound was a confined bird or rodent that sensed the earthquake and feared its dangerous captivity. Elle's recognition, however, directed me toward another interpretation. It was as if my father, who had been a good friend to me while he lived, briefly returned to give me a sign of outward terror to confirm the validity of my inner terror. He was saying to me, "You are right, son. This place is as dangerous as you think. You can be destroyed here."

After that difficult night, Elle and I spent many more days in Bali, and I struggled valiantly to understand the land and the people while keeping alive my brief moment of confusion about the nature of God. On our last day in the town of Blahbatuh we witnessed a mass cremation that the town had been preparing for many months. Cremations are Bali's most joyous events, for as flames lick corpses, souls are liberated from bodies and float above our demon-ridden world of suffering. Thus, standing wide-eyed in the graveyard among the celebrant citizens of Blahbatuh, I watched twenty-two bright-foil-decorated, animal-shaped sarcophagi blaze skyward, and, as the air filled with smoke and flakes of char and my nostrils ached with the smell of burning bone and flesh, I asked myself, "Am I being liberated or destroyed?"

When Elle and I came back to Maine, we were physically and spiritually exhausted. In the mornings before our return to work, I gathered eel grass from the shore and mulched our garden of beach roses, and on afternoon, we cruised the fresh bay waters and watched harbor seals fish around the ledges. In the open passages past the islands, droning lobster boats winched their traps from the weedy bottom while bright-colored spinnakers swelled and snapped in the breeze. With my hands in the soil of the garden or grasping the wheel of the boat, I felt alive, but, aside from these simple acts, I had no idea what had happened to me or what I would do. I particularly did not know how I would tell anyone the story of our failed pilgrimage to Bali.

Late one afternoon, as I worked among the roses, I turned over a clump of eel grass to discover a deep-blue mussel shell. The blueness made my heart glad, and I put the shell in my shirt pocket where it remained the next day as Elle and I traveled to the White Mountains for our climb up the King Ravine to Madison Spring Hut, an AMC shelter in the col between the peaks of Mt. Madison and Mt. Adams.

The climb was hard but beautiful. Streaks of clouds streamed over the ravine whose rim was richly colored with green lichen and tufts of lavender mountain azalea. Tired from the climb, we ate a hearty meal, retired early, and then rose the next morning to hike a short distance into the tundra-like col to Star Lake, a shallow basin of water, fed by springs and the moisture of passing clouds.

From a boil of quartz stone near the lake Elle and I looked down on the tea-colored water framed by ancient boulders and wavering fringes of red-tinged reeds and rushes. Behind us the orange-brown peak of Mr. Madison rose like a great, glowing pyramid, and suddenly I thought of the cinder cone of Gunung Agung. Just at that moment I remembered two stories that wove together the moment in the col, my confusion at Besakih, and the revelations of the Alaskan eclipse thirty years before.

The first was a recollection. In essence, on that day at Denali as I watched the sun blacken and nature turn on its head, I remembered that this remarkable vision of the heavens was unavailable to much of the world lying in the total eclipse zone because of an obliterating smudge of volcanic ash from the eruption of a huge volcano in the Indonesian archipelago. That volcano—smearing God's eye as I stood in Denali—was Gunung Agung.

 I was told the second story while in Bali. The eruption of Agung in March 1963 tragically corresponded with one of Bali's great festivals when her Hindu peoples make a pilgrimage to the most sacred temple. In the hours before thousands were to convene at the Mother Temple the volcano rumbled and hissed, and devotees grew worried. With anxiety they asked the priests what they should do, and the priests, convinced that piety would protect all from disaster, urged the people to come.

 It is hard to imagine what it must have been like when the crater blew, and fire and molten stone fell upon the people, burning and suffocating them, then hellishly sluicing its way down the mountain to incinerate villages below. The Mother Temple was burned and buried, only to be built again upon the same spot where I would come thirty years later for my brief moment of confusion about the nature of God.

 Reflecting on these two stories, I gazed at the beauty of Star Lake, rifting slightly in the mountain breeze and saw what had happened to me. At twenty, unconscious of the Mother, yet needing to meet Her, She revealed Herself in the noetic magic of a highly ordered world, roiled and calmed by a solar eclipse. At fifty, however, having forged a sturdy, prestigious, and financially rewarding life, I was forced, like an anxious, frightened Balinese supplicant, to stumble my way toward an alter where I would be burned and suffocated by forces beyond human understanding. The presence of the Mother was in both; both were needed for the journey.

 At twenty, I would be transfigured by a sensuous experience of great beauty where mystery opened my imagination to a dream of myself—all this as the smoke and ash belched out of Gunung, halfway around the world. At fifty, however, in a paradise billed to be extraordinarily imaginative, I would be stripped of all my imaginative powers. I would be emptied, mortified, and left in a vast vibrating darkness with only one feeble light—my brief moment of confusion about the nature of God. Then from that moment of confusion I would have to build a totally new basis for my faith or risk the soul calcification and death that goes with living an empty, but apparently intact and secure life.

Seeing it—the glory and mortification—I held Elle tight, and, as the light grew stronger, we watched the shadow of Mt. Adams slide across the col. From my shirt pocket I withdrew the deep blue mussel shell and pressed it into her hand. With reverence, she took Mother Ocean's shell and placed it under a stone by the quartz parapet overlooking Star Lake.

In the valley below us a dark plume arose from a papermill and then settled over the town in a thin brown haze. The smudge reminded me that there is no protection from the profane in the world, that pristine breaking forth of new life in Alaska is connected to fiery death on Agung. It also told me that East and West have interpenetrated each other, impregnated each other, corrupted each other, and sold each other to each other, and that there is absolutely no place on the planet where an aware individual is not faced with brief moments of confusion about the nature of God.

The mountain air was good for Elle and me, and it reminded us of the perfection that does lie in the human heart and the imagination's capacity to discern the Real. On this day we had offered the Mother of the Mountains the blue shell from the sea. From its place in the rose garden, we had carried it up the mountain to the cloud waters of Star Lake, and every step of the way we had been mindful of our precious moments on this imperiled planet. This same mindfulness we dedicated to every step back through the alpine gardens and down the glacial rubble of the ravine to the winding stream at its bottom and the road that would lead us home.

Walter Christie is assistant chief of psychiatry at Portland's Maine Medical Center.

TOM O'GRADY

I'm Told

♦

THERE ARE STARS beneath the sea,
that their dust, a handful of it, is as dense as Everest
and all those stories there, those scattered bones,
and the bright scarfs of the women on the shore
follow like the barren obsequy
that grips you as you sink beneath the sea.

Here, where the water is glass
you risk the touch of singing coral
lit by the penetrating sun as it waves
its bright star song to the dust below
until the broken clouds disclose and arrange
the makings of this place:
which is the making of you,
hovering, lost below:
small boy among the slender shadows
of Barracuda, small boy again.
Let no silver trinket flash in that soft light, I'm told.
Swirl near enough, but not to touch,
in water clear as air
and come back to see the star points
positioning in the night above,
lucid as breath.

Tom O'Grady is editor of the *Hampden–Sydney Poetry Review* and Poet-in-Residence at Hampden–Sydney College in Virginia.

PART II
Spiritual Living

◆

The spiritual level
is opened
by a love
toward the neighbor
and increases
through insights
into what is
true and good.

—ADAPTED FROM SWEDENBORG

ZALMAN SCHACHTER

Spiritual Eldering
Coming to Terms with Mortality

♦

THE WORK I'VE BEEN DOING lately is called Spiritual Eldering. Most of us in the midst of today's youth culture don't have the slightest idea how to be an 'elder'. Aging, as people think of it, is largely diminishing, since citizens of the United States currently don't see themselves as much alive after they're not in the saddle. Many people want to die in the saddle. The silliness of that is that they have plowed, they have sown the seed, but they've never harvested. Many people come into the elder years with extended lifespans, and, not having extended consciousness, they are dying longer, instead of living longer. If I had to live with the mentality of a forty-year-old, by the time I was sixty-five or seventy, I'm a loser. Because if I try to compete with a forty-year-old on the same level, I can't win. Rather, I have to own my diminishments. But if I'm not competing with the forty-year old, why don't I own my role in society according to my own special gifts and hard won wisdom? You see, we are bereft of elders in our society.

Now, how does one become an elder? Eldering is a process by which one uses the tools that the sacred traditions have given us. These tools are largely contemplative tools. You read something by Swedenborg and then what do you do? If you don't think about it, then it's stuff that you won't read again. It will all sound the same. If you read one book of the *Arcana,* it must be you've read them all. What's the use of having all these volumes? The answer is, if you read it, and you think about it and let you mind wander through the territory where it will take you, you have a fantastic preparation

---

Van Rijn, Rembrandt. *A Scholar in His Study, Watching a Magic Disk* ["Dr. Faustus"].
Etching, seventeenth century. Washington, D.C.: National Gallery of Art. Gift of R. Horace Gallatin, 1949.

and you want to read on because you have learned something, rather than just accumulated information.

Life needs finishing, it needs completion. None of us have the tools nor the plan by which we can complete life. What we get is a progressive uselessness that creeps up on us. We feel there is nothing more that we can do. So we're just hanging around, being warehoused, until it is time to say goodbye. Isn't there another and better way to die? This is what the search of all my work has been. It's asking people to do a difficult piece of work first: coming to terms with our mortality. Until I could come to terms with my own mortality, I had no future.

Let me give you an example. I'm here, and over there is the kitchen. As I turn to walk toward the future, I see something happening over there. The angel of death is waiting for me. So I don't want to see. I cut my mind off—my knowing off—from the future. Instead of walking to the future, I'm backing into the kitchen. And that's what we're all doing, you see? Unless we can walk like this—resolute—and say, look, look what a long line it is before I can even get into the row. There is plenty to do. But when you begin to take your consciousness and cloud it and diminish it, make it more and more opaque, you're backing into the kitchen. What do you see from the past if your back in the kitchen? Oy! This is what I did wrong, didn't do so well, the things I'm sorry about. This is where I lost it, and on and on. This is the time of life we fear, the time most of us don't want to get to do. So we have put these things that happened to us in life into different kinds of filing cabinets. There are some kinds of filing cabinets that cause us anxiety, so we don't like to open them up. Much of what is in the past, that is, in those filing cabinets we get anxious about and don't want to think about. We say "Do I want to think about this memory? I think not." We turn away from delving into the past.

So how many good filing cabinets do I have? Maybe two or three. How many others do I have? Many. Now what happens is that if I would dare to open some of the filing cabinets of the past, I would see that there I have some stocks and bonds that I thought were worthless and have grown very much in value. It's like the irritation of the oyster causing the pearl to be created. It's gut stuff.

So in the closets of the papers of the past, when I open them up and look at them with an eye of wisdom, an eye of the present for what I have learned in life, I find out that most of my successes were the results of the fallout of my failures. Think about that. I learned from what didn't work and where I failed, which led to different directions. That's what it means to see how grateful I am for my failures. So part of this work that we do in spiritual eldering is to try to get people to have this appreciation for their failures. It's when people come to join us to do this work and we teach them how to come to terms with mortality and how to open up the future by opening the past and allowing the human culture to talk, to act, to think.

I feel a huge interest in the theory: that there is a way that this work can be done, and that might have some bearing on your own spiritual process because the proof of the pudding in spirituality turns out to be how we handle the last part of life. When I divide life into seven-year periods, I get the January of life until age seven or so. The February of life is when puberty sets in. The March of life comes at twenty-one years or so, the April of life at twenty-eight. If you look at life in this form, then the years of the summer turn out to be July, August, September, and those are the months in which you are active in the world—in other words, from age forty to sixty. That's when you do your main thing. And then from sixty-three you begin to retire, to go into the October and November and December of life. Most people don't have a script of how to develop the spiritual self during that time. When you look at most of the writings, spiritual directives have been written for youth and for early age. The friend who wrote *Mirror for Simple Souls* or Brother Lawrence's *The Practice of the Presence of God*—these are authors of the kinds of books that are largely about the spiritual writing of younger people. But what of the spiritual writing of people who have no model?

This work is in the phase of what I call research and development. We're trying out new things. One is to give people the tools to do life's review, and another is to help life's completion. Those of you who have studied psychology know that Freud was talking about two instincts, the *libido,* the life instinct and the death instinct. I think what he called the death instinct *thanatos* is really the instinct for completion, not for death, but for completion. When I'm younger, I want to open up a lot of things, I want to try many, many options, but when I get older I want to reduce my options a little bit so I can complete some. When I was younger and I was alone, I felt lonely. Now when I'm alone I enjoy my solitude. It's like an attitude that elders have that's necessary to have. The spiritual that they seek is for completion.

When people talk about the brain in physiology, they tell you that we have a prehistoric part. That is to say, this first part of our brain structure deals with the dinosaur, my turf, my place, my food. The other part they call the limbic brain. That's the puppy dog part of us which is excited by or stimulated by noise, that loves to be with other people and to celebrate. The next part they call the cortex. The cortex is a part of the brain with which we have been operating up to now. That combination totals not more than fifteen percent of our brain capacity. What about the other eighty-five percent of the brain we haven't yet activated? This is why, when you're talking to people about aging, the extended life span requires extended consciousness. More of that brain capacity that wasn't ripened before, the green apple, makes something happen. Where you couldn't grow a decent apple, what you had were crab apples. Why? The summer was too short. You couldn't grow a decent apple. *I think you can't grow a decent human being in a short life span.* It takes so much to make an extended consciousness, a complete person; that what's being given to us now is the extended life span to grow the extra part. But we can't do it by being couch potatoes and watching television. It has to be done by doing, by exercising, by doing mind aerobics, as it were. I don't only mean the intellectual part of the mind, I also mean that part which is spiritual. The part you use for meditation and reflection.

There are levels of meditation that are like experiencing hot and cold. The mind gets cold, gets warm, and then it probably gets hot. You have a sense when you are zeroing in on truth in your meditation. It touches something very deep, and you make a commitment to that, and you make a covenant with that. That's basically the process, and the process is important along with the actualization.

I find that when people have done this work of the completion process that they're not fearing death so much, and there are two parts to that. One is that when I get to the place, finally, where I've made my peace with death, I lose the anxiety. Then I can ask myself the question: what do I need to do to complete—to finish. My experience as to what we do in response to this nagging question is that we gain energies and a sharper enjoyment of the present. Thus the sunset of our lives becomes a harvest of mellow delights.

Zalman Schachter–Shalomi was born in Poland in 1924, raised in Austria, and, then, fleeing Hitler, came to the U.S. in 1941. In his ecumenical search he encountered Swedenborg's *Arcana Coelestia,* which paralleled the tradition of the Kabbalah. Dr. Schacter received his doctorate in Hebrew Letters at Hebrew Union College, is professor emeritus at Temple University, and founder of the Spiritual Eldering Institute (7318 Germantown Avenue, Philadelphia, Pennsylvania).

♦ BARBARA CASEY ♦

Everything in Its Place

♦

MY GRANDPARENT'S FARM wasn't a big farm—at least not by midwestern standards. The Killebrew farm to the north boasted fifteen hundred acres of corn each year. And to the south, old man Benson and his two sons kept three combines running when it was wheat harvest time. So the thirty-three acres my grandparents owned wasn't much. And there was another difference. Where other farms were planted in one or two large crops each year, my grandparents preferred a variety in their order of things, using each acre to its maximum, often doubling up on purpose.

In this order, apple and cherry trees grew in the pastures where the cows grazed, offering fruits for canning and freezing, as well as shade for the cows. The pigs were kept in a pen near the place where my grandfather brought in the crops, thereby making it easy to feed the pigs those crops that were not marketable. And my grandmother's vegetable garden was a marvel in itself. Contained within a white picket fence, the garden was divided by a walkway of wooden planks, laid end to end.

Perpendicular to the walkway were rows of vegetables, each row bordered with a particular flower. The kind of flower and its color was determined by what vegetable grew near it and what insect the flower was to discourage. To protect the pole beans from June beetles, mixed colored zinnias were used. Bright yellow marigolds were planted to protect the tomato vines from the foliage-eating caterpillar. The scented geranium kept the pesky mosquito away. The fragrant sweetpea and sweet William attracted bees to help with pollination throughout the garden. I'm not sure what

---

Corot, Camille. *The Little Curious Girl*. Oil on board. Philadelphia Museum of Art. Mr. And Mrs. Walter H. Annenberg.

function the purple four o'clocks served, or the rather large bush in the corner whose small russet flower smelled like fresh strawberries, except that they were part of the overall order.

I was seven years old the summer my mother and I stayed with my grandparents. My father had been sent on a military assignment overseas, so mother thought it would be a good opportunity to spend some time with my grandparents and help out on the farm.

The first thing I learned was that there was always work to be done on a farm. Mother helped with cooking and cleaning while grandmother prepared vegetables picked from her garden for canning and freezing. I was given the responsibility of gathering eggs from the henhouse. Using a special egg basket, each afternoon at precisely five o'clock I would walk through my grandmother's garden, down to the end of the wooden planks, turn right, and go through a gate to the chicken yard. I really enjoyed gathering the eggs, and even though all the chickens looked basically alike, I soon learned to tell them apart (or at least I thought I could) and gave each one a name.

One hot afternoon, it seemed as though five o'clock would never arrive. Restless, I wandered through the gate of grandmother's garden and followed the boards to the end. Instead of turning right as usual when gathering eggs, I followed a worn dirt path leading behind grandmother's potting shed where she kept her gardening tools. I was surprised to find some blackberry vines full of juicy ripe berries growing on a fence behind the shed. After eating several, I continued on the dirt path until I came to a gate flanked on each side by tall spears of pink, white, and purple hollyhocks.

I pushed the gate open and walked into a red-bricked courtyard. Two white, shining buildings—one large and another small, stood at one end of the courtyard, and opposite them, in the shade of a spreading cottonwood tree, to the eyes of a seven-year-old girl, was a beautiful golden carriage hitched to two prancing white horses.

Every day after that, I returned to the courtyard to ride in the beautiful carriage. The horses were always hitched and ready to take me anywhere I wanted to go. Sometimes we would go on long journeys to places I had only heard of or read about. Other times we would simply stay in the courtyard, and I would brush their thick manes and tails. I never asked my grandparents about the horses and the golden carriage. Instead, I kept my secret, happily spending the long days of summer traveling to this place or that, always to return in time to gather eggs.

I don't know when I stopped thinking about the courtyard and the beautiful carriage. When my father returned from overseas, we were transferred to another military base. It was not until many years later that I returned to the farm.

◆

IN CELEBRATION of my grandparents' fiftieth wedding anniversary, I returned to the farm for a short visit, bringing along my five-year-old daughter. Even though I knew my grandparents had stopped tending their land years earlier, I wasn't prepared for how different everything would look. Everything seemed so much smaller than I remembered, and so much older. The order was more difficult to see.

On the day of the anniversary party, dressed and ready for the other guests to arrive, my daughter went outside to wait, with the instructions used by mothers everywhere ringing in her ears—"Don't wander off," and "Don't get dirty."

After a half hour or so my little girl came running into my room. Her eyes were wide with excitement and her hands and mouth had a tint of purple that suspiciously resembled blackberry juice.

"Mama, come quick. Hurry," she exclaimed, with the urgency that only a five-year-old can feel.

She pulled me out the back door and through the garden gate. Weeds had now taken over where the neat rows of vegetables and flowers had once grown. And the wooden planks were rotted, making it difficult to walk. But through the weeds we went, past the back of the old potting shed, and beyond the untamed brush of blackberry vines.

"We have to be careful with grandmother's roses," my daughter said, as she carefully exposed a gate behind a rather thick tangle of wild Queen Anne's lace and honeysuckle.

As we walked through the gate, I paused and looked around. The old barn and tool shed were weathered and gray, all the white paint long ago lost. The bricked courtyard itself was now hard-baked, interrupted by quack grass and many dandelions, and much of the fence surrounding the area was broken and decayed. An old wooden hay wagon, weathered gray like the barn and tool shed, was standing off to one side, rusted and its wheels leaning at peculiar angles.

My daughter, looking toward it, clasped her stained hands together and exclaimed, "Isn't it beautiful!" Then, using the spokes of one wheel as a ladder, she carefully climbed into the wagon.

"It's a carriage," she stated matter-of-factly, as she peered down over the side.

I looked at my daughter's happy face and realized that, just as another child had many years earlier, she had discovered the order of my grandparents' farm. Her dress had blackberry stains, and her hair mussed. But there would be plenty of time later to take care of that. For the moment, there was something more important to do. Two prancing white horses were waiting to carry a princess to her destination in a beautiful golden carriage.

Barbara Casey is the author of two novels for children, and her poetry and stories for adults have appeared nationally in magazines and newspapers. Ms. Casey is the Florida Regional Advisor for the Society of Children's Book Writers and Illustrators.

♦ ROSE ROSBERG ♦

Offerings of Chaos

♦

DON'T APOLOGIZE, weather forecaster,
we're aware of out-of-the-blue
shifts in air currents,
                              hobo tricks
starting intricate patterns.

                              Straight lines
are dull. Zigzag lightning
across breath-held threatening sky
flashes its own justification,
                              like a lover's kiss.

Neurologists suppose that brain cells
must dare irregular leaps in order
to birth original insights.

                              A fertile disorder
must spawn those stubborn seekers intent
on catching equations evasive as flies.

Rose Rosberg, a New York City poet, has recently had poetry collections published by Singular Speech Press (*Breathe In, Beathe Out,* 1992) and by Aegean Press (*The Country of Connections,* 1993). Her poems have appeared in many magazines.

◆ PENNY PAGLIARO ◆

Stopping at Ewa

◆

THERE ARE TIMES when people are dropped into the middle of a remarkable situation and are able to watch it unfold. It doesn't happen often, but it happened to me.

Ewa, pronounced "eva," is an old country town in Hawaii that has become so much a part of the island reality that it now serves a broader directional purpose, replacing the more precise "west" as a compass point. "It's ewa of the shopping center," the residents say, or, as my high-school students used to tell me, their absent classmate has "gone ewa," a place so far it was beyond imagining.

Founded in 1890, near the end of the great expansion of Hawaii's sugar industry, Ewa Plantation was one of the last in the vast network of plantations that covered the Islands. An old community by Hawaii standards, people assumed Ewa would be there forever.

It was started at a time when immigrant laborers were being hired and transported from all over the world to provide the necessary hands for planting, growing, and harvesting sugar cane. From China, Japan, the Philippines, Puerto Rico, Spain, Germany, Portugal, California, workers left behind family and friends to make their living in the cane fields.

Although legally structured as corporations, the nineteenth-century plantations were really feudal organizations. The plantation manager, often descended from a New England missionary family, held absolute power. Directly under him were skilled employees—chemists, engineers, and technicians—who battled each day to keep the fields and the sugar mill in high production. At the bottom of the ladder were the unskilled laborers, the field hands who dealt with the harsh physical

---

Olivier, Leah. *Hawaiian Sugar-cane Field.* Pen-and-ink drawing, 1995.

demands of this labor-intensive crop. The manager answered only to the board of directors.

Maintaining a stable labor force was probably the most critical problem of this industry. When plantation managers realized that family men made a more stable work force than bachelor laborers, they began offering family housing. This change along with free medical care, schooling, and subsidized retail goods, made plantations a good place to raise a family. Soon the transience of the plantation camps was replaced by permanent communities with schools, churches, stores, and shared experiences. Children were born, grew up, married, and died on the plantation.

At its peak, Ewa Plantation was home to five-thousand employees and their dependents, clustered in villages or "camps" generally based on ethnic origins. There was Filipino Camp, Japanese Camp, Pipe Line Camp (Spanish), Portuguese Camp, sometimes two or three camps for each ethnic group. In these camps, families far away from home could still retain some semblance of cultural comfort. The skilled workers and the manager lived in Haole (Caucasian) Camp, and they were always white, regardless of their country of origin.

The house a plantation worker occupied reflected the worker's occupation and social standing. The manager lived in the largest, most impressive home, and at Ewa, the manager's house is still the only two-story residence. Skilled workers enjoyed comfortable bungalows with generous yards, meticulously manicured. Unskilled workers raised their families in smaller cottages, although an addition to the family often brought a move to larger quarters. Each cottage had a garden where tropical fruits and vegetables were grown for family use. If the entrepreneurial managed to sell their extra produce, no one objected.

Ewa quickly became a showplace for the sugar industry. Closest to Honolulu—two hours or so by the old Oahu Railway—Ewa was the plantation to which all visiting dignitaries were taken as an example of the civility of Hawaii's plantation system. Great strides were made there in plantation agriculture and infant medical care. Dr. and Mrs. George Bernard Shaw visited. Eleanor Roosevelt came and stayed in the guest cottage behind the manager's home.

During the 1930s, formal parties, were hosted by the manager every month; tuxedos were required.

I discovered Ewa near the end of its glory, in the late 1960s, my young family and I were living in a nearby town established by the plantation for the benefit of its retirees (and later occupied by non-plantation newcomers like us). The road that connected our beach community to jobs in Honolulu bypassed Ewa Plantation, and every day a discreet sign on the highway pointed down a narrow road.

"EWA," it announced.

One Sunday afternoon, when we finally took time to explore, I could hardly believe my eyes. The narrow country road parted a green sea of sugar cane and took me from the present to a way of life long past. Before me lay a tranquil village, not quite Brigadoon, but just as remarkable.

Banyan trees arched over the road, and children played easily along its margins. The Catholic Church and the Congregational Church stood watch on either side of Ewa Elementary School. The neat white bungalows and carefully trimmed lawns of Renton Village ("haole camp") seemed to say, "We belong here. Who are you?"

Dominating everything was the sugar mill, its twin red and white smoke stacks, the rigid standard-bearers that proclaimed the business of this community, Ewa Plantation Company, a sign announced.

In the shadow of the mill stood the Administration Building and Ewa Shopping Basket, the plantation's general store, two graceful structures built during the 1930s when sugar managed to produce substantial profits despite the Great Depression. The nearby recreation center and baseball diamond were busy with activity.

Beyond Renton Village lay Mill Village and Tenney Village, then Verona Village, the small cottages and gardens of each often revealing not only the status, but also the culture of its occupant. Japanese bonsai and orchids, Filipino fruits and vegetables, fighting chickens and country dogs presented the rich mix of difference that has come to typify Hawaii.

My overwhelming impression of the plantation as we drove through was its serenity. Structure and order were present in large supply, indicating a firm hand at work behind the scenes. No building lacked a fresh coat of paint. Each was in good repair. Windows sparkled.

There is a certain seductiveness in imposed order, and I suspect that my own longing for calm and tranquillity added dimension to what I saw at Ewa that day. Compared with the storm of social unrest plaguing America in the late 1960s and the violence of the war in Vietnam, Ewa seemed to me a quiet cove where life went on much as it had for decades. Years later, I learned that in the early days of the plantation, guards stood watch at the gates, not to keep the workers in but to keep intruders out. Ewa must have seemed a safe harbor to others as well.

These impressions stayed in my memory for years. A change of residence, two children, career, divorce, and other surprises did nothing to dim them. My life moved on, but, Ewa, when I gave it any thought at all, was frozen in time.

It was nearly twenty years before I returned. In 1987, having enrolled in a new graduate program in historic preservation at the University of Hawaii, I had begun to look at my community with a different perspective. On a rainy Sunday afternoon, a fellow graduate student and I decided to see what had become of Ewa Plantation.

Driving down the rain-soaked road, it was obvious that something was terribly wrong. In place of sugar cane, the windshield wipers cleared and then blurred two new housing developments.

When we entered Renton Village, I blinked in disbelief. The neat bungalows had become derelict, with sagging roofs and unpainted walls. Some buildings had collapsed or been bulldozed. The recreation center was gone, burned to the ground. Mill Village had disappeared. Rubbish was strewn along the rutted roads. Grass, weeds, and abandoned cars were everywhere. People were still living there, we could tell, but the villages had become a sad setting for their lives.

Worst of all, the sugar mill had vanished, its towering smoke stacks silenced.

Even through a rain-spattered window, it was plain to see Ewa was dying. What could have happened? As we drove away, my friend and I agreed something had to be done or Ewa was doomed.

I once heard someone say that coming upon a situation like this is like passing an accident on the freeway. You always expect someone else to stop and render aid. However, when you look around and no one else is there, you know it's your turn.

It took me a while to figure this out.

In the meantime, I began doing research. I discovered that due to increased competition from foreign sugar, costs of union labor, and other factors, Ewa Plantation had closed in 1970, much to the surprise of its employees.

The villages and cane fields had subsequently been rented to a rival plantation, Oahu Sugar Company, with the understanding that the former Ewa laborers and retirees would be allowed to stay on in their cottages.

But there were differences between Ewa Plantation and Oahu Sugar, whose policies did not include pride of place. With little maintenance, the old villages began to deteriorate quickly in the tropical climate.

Beyond that, an insider whispered, Oahu Sugar and the landowner, Campbell Estates, had a quiet agreement that, when the agricultural lease expired in 1996, Oahu Sugar would return the land to Campbell Estates bare of all improvements.

That stopped me cold. All the villages would be bulldozed. The residents would be moved out. Ewa would simply disappear.

The cane fields around Ewa were already being rezoned for residential use, and forty-thousand homes were planned. Nearly one hundred years of Hawaii's unique plantation history were at stake, and, with them, the relationships of an entire community were at risk, as well.

This is wrong, I kept saying to myself. Wrong thinking, wrong planning, wrong values, just plain wrong. To wipe out an established community in order to build anonymous housing subdivisions is not only wrong, muddle-headed.

A few of my classmates took on Ewa research projects of their own. An inventory of the "housing stock"—nearly 280 homes that had so far escaped the bulldozer—led to a map of the villages with dates of construction. A landscape survey documented the trees, flowers, and gardens which had been added by generations of Ewa residents. By the time our research was completed, there were enough measured drawings, photos, and most of the support needed to nominate Ewa's villages to the National Register of Historic Places.

Slowly, Ewa emerged from the shadows of its past to become an historic preservation project of national importance. The question was, who was going to take it on? Surely, I thought, someone will show up, someone who has experience in rescuing towns, someone who knows what they're doing, someone else.

After a year of waiting, I realized that this was the accident on the freeway, there was no one else around, and my turn had come. I had become *the somebody else*.

Late in January 1989, I invited to my home, a few classmates, a concerned Ewa resident, a woman born and raised on Ewa Plantation who had strong ties to the past and to present community members, others who had expressed interest generated from a newspaper article, and the director of the University of Hawaii's historic preservation program.

By the end of the afternoon, we had agreed on what we wanted to accomplish: first, to make sure that the current residents had a chance to buy the homes they had only been allowed to rent and, second, to restore and preserve the villages for the future.

Two of the three attorneys in our group volunteered to file the documents necessary to register us as a nonprofit corporation. I agreed to be president. We soon had a name: Friends For Ewa. Within days, we started signing up members.

Suddenly, we were swept into a whirlpool of activity that was unlike anything I had ever experienced. Within two months, we had over 250 members and a mailing list of nearly a thousand. Our supporters came from Ewa and beyond, and from both the present and the past. By igniting a spark of possibility, it seemed we had lit a skyrocket of hope.

The heart of the community, we discovered, was still beating. Help came from everywhere, and our ranks of active volunteers grew quickly. We persuaded. We petitioned. We kanoodled. No one escaped. Politicians, businessmen, union leaders, federal officials, national and international preservationists—and most importantly, ordinary people like us—heard the message from Ewa.

We discovered that the City and County of Honolulu had plans to widen Renton Road, Ewa's main street, and use it as a major thoroughfare for the new subdivisions nearby. This would have had a devastating impact on the quiet villages. We called our first public meeting and got over two-hundred signatures on a petition to stop the widening project. To our astonishment, the City halted its plans. It was our first success. Soon, all but the most pessimistic began to admit the possibility of improvement.

The media loved us, and we encouraged their affection. Ewa and its hard working immigrant residents made the best kind of human interest story, and every event we sponsored caught the attention of television or newspaper reporters. Since we had neither money nor power, we relied heavily on public opinion. And as every politician knows, public opinion means votes.

The bulldozing, however, continued despite our efforts to secure a moratorium. Then, through a series of remarkable coincidences, we got help from the chief executive of the corporation that owned Oahu Sugar. He mandated that demolition be stopped until a complete evaluation could be done. We were excited, encouraged, and stunned.

In the meantime, the City and County of Honolulu had become interested in Ewa as a possible "affordable housing" project, but early plans put forward by the City were even more frightening than the bulldozer. Their proposal packed in 2,700 houses where 280 now stood. Back and forth we went, see-sawing between success and failure.

When summer 1989 came and Ewa's children were out of school, other problems arose. Within ninety days, forty-five fires were set in Ewa. Fire was a horrifying threat in this wood frame community, especially to the elderly and infirm. When they weren't setting fires, bored teenagers raced stolen cars through the villages, terrorizing the elders. Fire trucks and police cars were called to Ewa on a regular basis, but never in time to stop the mischief.

I had been prepared to deal with rural problems but found Friends For Ewa now confronted with problems I associated with the inner city. Then it dawned on me that this was neither an inner city nor a suburban or country problem but the problem of children who had no sense of belonging and no sense of their own value to their community.

Some of our volunteers organized the elders into a Neighborhood Watch, and a creative, dynamic Ewa minister started a youth activity program at his church that cut to the heart of the situation. Within a year, fires and terrorism virtually disappeared.

Someone observed that the centennial anniversary of Ewa Plantation's founding was coming up. We started planning a major celebration almost immediately, and when the weekend event finally took place in August 1990, many familiar faces appeared.

The Governor spoke. The Congressional delegation spoke. Local politicians spoke. Business leaders spoke. But the strongest message came from more than 5,000 past and present residents from all over the United States who had come home to Ewa once more. Despite time, distance, and the uncertainties of life, they were still connected to this tiny community by the cords of their shared memories.

The media captured it all.

The day after the centennial celebration, Ewa had become everyone's favorite cause. Within months, the City and County of Honolulu's plans for Ewa crystallized into a comprehensive plan to revitalize and preserve the community, protect its historic heritage, and offer the houses to the current residents at cost. Professional preservation consultants were hired to help with the planning, and the City began pioneering its first historic preservation housing project.

Transitions are hard, no matter how well planned or well intentioned. The transition from the feudal order of the old plantation to a self-governing, democratic community ready to face the twenty-first century has been a challenge for Ewa. Now, in 1995, the work is still in progress.

As I write this, the roads in Ewa are torn up for a new sewer system. Dust and confusion and an uncertain completion date have discouraged some Ewa residents. A few have moved away. Some are frustrated that improvements are taking so long. Others are uncomfortable with the inevitable changes they see coming; Ewa will never again be the way it was when the plantation manager was in charge.

The alternative, however, is even less appealing. With success almost at hand, it is easy to forget how close Ewa came to obliteration.

I wonder what would have happened if, more than seventy years ago, the plantation manager had been concerned with crops but not with people. What if he had not taken steps to stabilize the workforce, had not seen that family life was good for profits, had not made the well-being of plantation children a priority? Would the plantation have survived?

Probably not. Communities that fail to invest in people, fail. Certainly the children of Ewa, many now gray-haired, remember their hometown not as a place of commerce where they happened to live, but as a place filled with friends and family who happened to work for the same company. They are tied by shared memories. It gives them balance and a sense of continuity.

Some time ago, I decided that Ewa was in good hands and that I needed to move along. At a farewell party, a young woman late in her first pregnancy said, "You know, my great-grandfather came from Japan to work in the fields at Ewa. My grandfather and my father were born and raised at Ewa. I was born and raised at Ewa. Now, my child can be born and raised at Ewa."

When I remember Ewa now, I remember that woman and her child and the continuity they represent.

I'm glad I stopped to help. . . .

When not working on historic preservation projects, **Penny Pagliaro** runs her own commercial real estate brokerage company. She has lived in Hawaii since 1965.

♦ GEORGE F. DOLE ♦

Is Good Citizenship Dual Citizenship?
Swedenborg's Two Worlds

♦

IN EIGHTEENTH-CENTURY EUROPEAN MONARCHIES, it was taken for granted that the church legitimized the monarch and that the state supported the church—British coinage still informs us that Elizabeth is queen "by the grace of God" and is also "defender of the faith." This mutually supportive relationship between church and state implied an equally close link between theological irregularity and political sedition. When one of Swedenborg's earliest followers, Dr. Gabriel Beyer, was accused of heresy for his "Swedenborgianism," his defense included the observation that Swedenborg's theology would lead people to be excellent citizens.[1]

As a full-time public servant and a member of the College of Mines—roughly the equivalent of our Department of the Interior—Swedenborg labored faithfully and ably to modernize Sweden's mining and metallurgical industries, the principal foundations of her prosperity and security. As a diligent member of the House of Lords, he displayed a determination to stabilize his country's currency,[2] and wrote memoranda on foreign trade and foreign policy.[3]

Unquestionably, the onset of his spiritual experiences made an immense change in his thinking and in his life, but Swedenborg's civic interest and commitment did not disappear. While he eventually resigned from the College of Mines, he remained as active as ever in the House of Lords. In 1771, just a year before his death, he dusted off a memorandum on fiscal policy that he had written in 1722, updated and annotated it copiously, and had it published.[4]

Emanuel Swedenborg (left), 1688–1772, was among the great scholars who grew out of the Enlightenment, men whose minds were charged with a vital spirit of inquiry. He wrote, with a quill pen, more than a hundred volumes: first scientific, then philosophical, and finally theological.

His interest in citizenship was deep, and comes out explicitly in his theology. It may seem at times submerged in his exploration of the spiritual transformation of the individual, but Swedenborg frequently calls attention to the importance of citizenship.

> It is commonly said that we are all neighbors to ourselves—that is, that we look to our own welfare first of all. The doctrine of charity teaches us how this works. We are our own neighbors, true, but last of all rather than first of all. A higher priority is given to others who are constructively engaged, and a still higher priority to the larger community.[5]

But by putting the community first, Swedenborg was not advocating the sacrifice of the individual. That is not at all what his heaven is about.

> Mutual love in heaven consists of loving the neighbor more than one's self, with the result that the whole heaven presents itself as a kind of single individual. Through mutual love from God, all the individuals are bound together in community, which is why the happiness of all is communicated to each one, and the happiness of each one to all. The very form of heaven is of such a nature that each individual is like a kind of center, particularly a center of happiness from everyone.[6]

What comes immediately to mind is the irresistible lifting of spirits that comes in the presence of people whose joy is spontaneous and overflowing. To place the welfare of the community above that of the individual is to labor for the kind of community that cares for its individual members—its neighbors. The community that does not reflect this kind of care is more Moloch than neighbor. Like that fearful deity, it consumes rather than nurtures the individual.

Swedenborg's pragmatism comes to the fore in his frequent emphasis on constructive living, on "uses."

> By uses we mean not only the necessities of life . . . for one's self and one's own; but also the good of our country, of the community, and of our fellow-citizen. Merchandising is such a good when the love of it is the end, and money is a mediate, subservient love, provided the businessman rejects fraud and dishonest devices, disapproving of them as sins.[7]

As an example of uses in our own century, St. Francis House, a Boston day shelter for the homeless, could not provide its services for the good of others without the useful work of people who provide electrical and telephone service, maintain the vans that pick up clothing, transport the employees and volunteers, and the like. They in turn could not provide these services at any reasonable price if their sole purpose were to support St. Francis House. The system works—the homeless are served—to the extent that a great many people are useful and do their particular jobs well for the sake of doing them well and for the good of others. There is an intricate fabric of services, of "uses," which can be brought to focus on particular needs. This, I believe, is the kind of dynamic Swedenborg has in mind in statements such as the following:

> No one is wise, or lives, for self alone. . . . To live for others is to do uses. Uses are the bonds of society, which are as many in number as there are good uses; and uses are infinite in number.[8]

"Doing uses" (usus facere) might well be translated "providing services." It is this fabric of mutual service that is the essence of societal cohesion.

Swedenborgian theology, as Wilson Van Dusen has observed, at first glance does not seem to offer a specific discipline for personal transformation. Comparison with Eastern religions makes this inescapably clear. But, says Van Dusen, even though there is no specific discipline comparable to those of Buddhism or the martial arts or Tai Chi, there is the path of "uses" in Swedenborgianism.[9] On the subject of spiritual disciplines, Swedenborg challenges exclusive reliance on an ascetical lifestyle:

> Some people think that living a life that leads to heaven—a life called "spiritual"—is hard, because they have heard that you have to give up the world and strip yourself of all "fleshly" desires and "live spiritually." . . . The reality is completely different. . . . People who "live spiritually" in this fashion take on a mournful quality of life, one that is not open to heavenly delight. . . . If we are to accept heavenly life, we must by all means live in the world, involved in its dealings and affairs. Then, by living a moral and civic life we are accepting spiritual life. . . . Living an inner life without living an outward one at the same time is like living in a house without a foundation.[10]

One of the weakest points in Eastern spiritualities, I believe, is to be found in their tendency toward social and material inactivism, a tendency to accept one's lot in life with a sense of karmic fatalism.

The Christian idea of love to the neighbor rests on the assumption that our decisions do make a difference; we can make things better for those we care about.

Is the only truly good citizenship dual citizenship—a foot in both worlds? Civic responsibility will not be met squarely if the inner motivation is essentially self-serving. Spiritual transformation will be illusory unless it is grounded in the way we treat each other. Spiritual concerns include material concerns, as expressed by Swedenborg in the following passage:

> "Good uses" are to provide the necessities of life for oneself and one's own. They include wanting wealth for the sake of one's country and one's neighbor, whom wealthy people can help in far more ways than poor people can. . . . These uses are good to the extent that they have something divine within them, that is, to the extent that we focus on the divine and on heaven and make them our good, with wealth as no more than a subservient good.[11]

Oftentimes social justice seems to assert that all virtue lies with the poor and all vice with the rich. This rests, I would suggest, on a simplistic equation of "poor" with "oppressed" and "rich" with "oppressor." Even the poor, as the wealthy, need to temper their actions with good intentions. Otherwise, if given the opportunity, the poor will move from being the oppressed to being the oppressors. Swedenborg would disagree completely with Gladstone's dictum, however, that "power corrupts, and absolute power corrupts absolutely," if only on the grounds that God is omnipotent and incorruptible. It is not the amount of power that is at issue, but its quality. The Gospels advise that people who practice faithfulness or unfaithfulness in things least will do the same in things greatest.

But what about the goals—the good intentions—of a nation? Of what use to the world are we as a nation? In Swedenborgian terms, we might regard our nation as serving a "general use." Our inexorable progress toward a global economy and a global information community might be such a general use. The idealism of a century ago saw the United States, as a bulwark of political and intellectual freedom and, therefore, of scientific progress. It was a romantic ideal, in significant ways at odds with other realities, but at least it was an ideal. But where as a nation do we go from here? The answer rests on the priorities of individuals who are the foundation and life of the nation.

> For every general use is composed of innumerable ones, which are called mediate, administering, and subservient uses. All of them are [in heaven] coordinated and subordinated according to Divine order, and taken together, they constitute and perfect the general use, which is the common good.[12]

This is a statement about priorities in heaven. It is not necessarily an "other-worldly" statement. To the extent that we are citizens of that heavenly realm, giving our attention and our allegiance to "the general use which is the common good," our earthly citizenship has a chance to be truly constructive. Conversely, only the practice of responsible citizenship in this world awakens us to the beauty of heavenly community. Ultimately, it is either dual citizenship or no citizenship at all.

George F. Dole, who holds degrees from Yale, Harvard, and Oxford universities, teaches at the Swedenborgian seminary in Boston and summers in Maine. Besides teaching, Dr. Dole edits *Swedenborg Studies,* the Swedenborg Foundation's monograph series, and has written filmscripts.

Notes

1. Tafel, Rudolf L., ed. *Documents Concerning the Life and Character of Emanuel Swedenborg.* 2 v., bound as 3. London: Swedenborg Society, 1875, 1877.
2. Swedenborg, E. Swedenborg's Modest Thoughts on the Deflation and Inflation of Swedish Coinage. In *Studia Swedenborgiana,* edited by George F. Dole.6(2): 7–21, January 1987.
3. Woofenden, William Ross. *Swedenborg Researcher's Manual: A Research Reference Manual for Writers of Academic Dissertations, and for Other Scholars.* Bryn Athyn, Pennsylvania: Swedenborg Scientific Association, 1988. pp. 35, 44 for references.
4. *Ibid.* p. 113, for full reference.
5. Swedenborg, Emanuel. *Arcana Coelestia: The Heavenly Arcana Contained in the Holy Scripture or Word of the Lord Unfolded.* In *Genesis and Exodus.* 12 v. New York: Swedenborg Foundation,

1916. Paragraph 6933. As is customary in Swedenborgian studies, references to his theological works are not to pages but to paragraph numbers, which are uniform in all editions.
6. Swedenborg, Emanuel. *Arcana Coelestia*, Paragraph 2057.
7. Swedenborg, Emanuel. *Divine Providence*. New York, Swedenborg Foundation, 1963. Paragraph 220.
8. Swedenborg, Emanuel. *The Delights of Wisdom pertaining to Conjugial Love, after which follow the Pleasures of Insanity pertaining to Scortatory Love*. Samuel Warren, trans. New York: Swedenborg Foundation, 1915. Reprints, Paragraph 18.
9. Van Dusen, Wilson. *Uses: A Way of Personal Spiritual Growth*. New York: Swedenborg Foundation, 1978.
10. Swedenborg, Emanuel. *Heaven and Its Wonders and Hell: From Things Heard and Seen*. J. C. Ager, trans. New York: Swedenborg Foundation, 1900. Reprints, Paragraph 528.
11. *Ibid*. Paragraph 361.
12. *Ibid*. Paragraph 392.

Bibliography

Swedenborg, Emanuel. *Angelic Wisdom about Divine Providence*. William F. Wunsch, trans. New York: Swedenborg Foundation, 1963. Reprints.

———. *Arcana Coelestia: The Heavenly Arcana Contained in the Holy Scripture or Word of the Lord Unfolded, in Genesis and Exodus*. 12 v. New York: Swedenborg Foundation, 1916.

———. *The Delights of Wisdom Pertaining to Conjugial Love: After Which Follow the Pleasures of Insanity Pertaining to Scortatory Love*. Samuel Warren, trans. New York: Swedenborg Foundation, 1915.

———. *Heaven and Its Wonders and Hell: From Things Heard and Seen*. J. C. Ager, trans. New York: Swedenborg Foundation, 1900.

———. Swedenborg's Modest Thoughts on the Deflation and Inflation of Swedish Coinage. *Studia Swedenborgiana.*, edited by George F. Dole. 6: January 1987.

Tafel, Rudolf L., ed. *Documents Concerning the Life and Character of Emanuel Swedenborg*. 2 v., bound as 3. London: Swedenborg Society, 1875, 1877.

Van Dusen, Wilson. *Uses: A Way of Personal Spiritual Growth*. New York, Swedenborg Foundation, 1978.

Woofenden, William Ross. *Swedenborg Researcher's Manual: A Research Reference Manual for Writers of Academic Dissertations, and for Other Scholars*. Bryn Athyn, Pennsylvania: Swedenborg Scientific Association, 1988.

ROBERT LAWSON

Whaling Blood

♦

AT THE MOUTH OF THE RIVER, collectors
reach into the surf for the great teeth
of the Cretaceous shark.

Trousered legs in the sand,
they flash their catch.
But I have the whale's ear.

More dear than family scrimshaw,
shaped like a child's fist,
I hold the warm bone in my hand.

Placing his shelled ear to mine,
I hear the trembling roots of mountains
and the wash of missing men.

I know my Nantucket blood,
with nothing keeping it from the black tide
but blind luck, understands.

Every day we hunt what breaches from the dark,
sell off our casks of light,
and then return to the sea, empty-handed.

Robert Lawson is an editor for Macmillan Publishing. Before launching into computer book publishing, Rob was an English and history secondary-school educator.

Wyeth, Jamie. *Wolfbane*. Watercolor and ink on paper, 1984.
Chadds Ford, Pennsylvania: Brandywine River Museum. Museum Purchase.

♦ ISRAEL REA ♦

The Water's Edge

♦

WHEN NOAH reached the water's edge he waded right in, even with his new high-top sneakers he'd saved up to buy. The cold October water was halfway up his thighs before he reached his little sister who was screaming for him to leave her alone. "Just get away, you idiot!" her face contorted in rage.

"There's nothin' I'd like better than to see your sorry face goin' down for the last time." By now the water was above his waist, and his new shoes were being sucked into the pond's silt, "but if I let you drown Dad'll kill me." He grabbed her plastic inflatable raft with a grip that his sister could not loosen. He knew that he should have taken off his new shoes—that little voice had told him, but he hadn't and now they were most probably ruined.

They reached the water's edge where Noah pulled the raft onto the crushed grass, and his sister threw herself onto the soggy shore and wept. "I notice you're mostly dry," he said as he quickly glanced over her. "You may notice that I am not." This threw her into greater shrieks of sorrow and repentance.

"I'm sorry Noah, I promise I'll never do it again."

Noah fervently wished this to be true, but was afraid that it was not. He gathered up the raft and began the ascent to the house watching to see that his sister followed. He opened the back door for her as she entered before him. Her skinny back was hidden beneath her long brown hair.

"Now, listen Mariah, you can't keep tryin' to drown yourself or jump off the roof like last time. I might not be there to save ya."

"I could'a swum back."

"Like last time when it took me five minutes to find you in that black water and tryin' to revive you, thinking we'd lost you for sure, and then you began to puke all over me?"

"You would bring that up, wouldn't you"?

"I've got to tell Dad this time."

"Please Noah, if you tell him, they'll take me away again." He knew she spoke the truth, and that it would be a calamity.

"Why do ya have ta be so miserable all the time Mariah?" he asked as he pulled off his first shoe.

"I'm not!" The kitchen door slammed behind her.

The television come on as he put his new shoes and wet clothes into the washing machine. His father would be home no sooner than seven and was sometimes later if he had to work late. He thought he'd make macaroni and cheese for dinner. Noah thought longingly about his mother and how it would be different. First of all Mariah wouldn't have tried to drown herself because that hadn't started until Mom had passed away. Secondly, they probably could have expected fried chicken, homemade mashed potatoes, and biscuits. For dessert a peach cobbler, and all he'd had to do would be to help with the dishes. He didn't mind watching Mariah and doing most of the housework; he just wished she was here—that's all. Right now she'd be typing on her computer while she asked him about his day. She had a newspaper column called *Just Ask Marcelle*. People asked her about anything, but her favorite topic was gardening. Even if someone wrote in about getting a divorce, she'd end up comparing it to selective breeding or something. She got a lot of awards for her column, and they had gotten thousands of letters after she died.

Noah left the washing machine behind him. He could hear it filling with water. Should he have used cold water, he wondered? These were some of things his mother could answer. Maybe she'd written about pond slime in one of her articles. Hurriedly he ran to his room, threw on some clothes, and went back to her computer that still sat in the kitchen as if she'd left yesterday. Noah had his own computer in his room, his father had one at the office, and Mariah never used one anymore, so his mother's hadn't been used probably since the day she'd died.

Poking out from beneath the keyboard was the edge of a small, yellow piece of paper, he lifted the keyboard up and read the note.

"I've gone to get my hair cut. Back soon. Mom. " Her handwriting was sloppy as ever—as if she was still alive.

The first thing he pulled up onto the screen was her Word Perfect file. What caught his eye was pchcbl/wp. Maybe this was her peach cobbler recipe. He double-clicked the mouse, and this is what came up:

> Dear My Husband Is Slipping Away, First of all no matter how bad the situation may look at the moment my motto is—Never Give Up! It's like my twenty-year-old crepe myrtle bush that appeared dead as a doornail early last summer. I had its rootball practically dynamited out this last year, then manicured the ground and planted Rebel Fescue when what popped up? That's right—three little crepe myrtles. I was so pleased to see even a remnant of my old friend that every time I pass by those growing branches I am delighted.
>
> It's the same thing for your Lothario. I understand you feel you lost your looks with the passing of your third afterbirth and that your daughter's boyfriend has green hair and thinks that not picking his nose when the mood strikes is a white middle-class inhibition, but still I say—It's Not Dead Yet! Before you blast him out of the house try one more time. (Do blast the boyfriend out.) Let me tell you—divorce court sucks, and you and your children won't come out ahead. Try this peach cobbler recipe and do your best to see him the way you did when you were first married. Then if all else fails, start Xeroxing all his financial papers and call a divorce lawyer. Good luck. Marcelle.

Noah had read his mother's columns before and knew what he could expect. There, following her pen name, was the actual recipe. He turned on the printer and printed it out. But before he turned the computer off he glanced over her orderly files and saw qt5 and out of curiosity double clicked, and this is what came up: "4:45 Hair cut, tell N. to cut grass." Noah read this through ten times before printing it out as well.

It didn't make sense. His mother had died midwinter, and this was her last entry in a diary sub-file. This had to have been written recently. But no one had touched the computer for months. Noah went into the television room and asked Mariah, "Have you used Mom's computer?"

"Right."

Mariah was in her usual position on the sofa, covered with what was left of blue-plaid blanket and watching a program that the audience on television found hysterical even if Mariah didn't. "Look at this note," Noah said. "I found it in Mom's diary." Mariah was familiar with her mother's computer diary, so after reading it she responded.

"So?" Mariah's hands couldn't hold the note still after reading it, instead her fingers flipped the paper back and forth many times and began to fold it over. Noah watched as his sister folded it over and over again until it was the size of a quarter. She then began to unfold it—he knew this was so she could refold it again and again.

"So, this must've been written after she died." His sister did not look into her brother's dark eyes. He stood there with his rugby t-shirt on over a pair of baggy jeans looking somewhat more joyful than he had in the past six months. Mariah knew this was only temporary. "Dad must've written it," she answered as she began to rip off any corners of the note which stuck out unevenly.

"No way. I'll call and see." Noah picked up the phone from beside her, dialed his father's office number, and spoke to him briefly before hanging up. "He hasn't touched it."

He fell onto the sofa beside her and said, "You know there were other strange things too."

"Whad'ya mean?" By now the paper had become a scrap.

"Well, I heard Aunt Margaret say how she couldn't understand how come so many of Mom's clothes were missing."

"What clothes?"

"Like her favorite blue T-shirt for the garden."

"She probably threw that old holey thing away." Mariah thought longingly about her mother for a moment. If only she would walk in the door with that old shirt and holler for someone to come out and help her instead of sitting around doing nothing. Mariah's lap and the sofa were now covered with shreds of the paper Noah had given her.

"And the floppy disks of her copied files, we never could find them for that publisher."

"True, but they might still turn up."

"Are you kidding? The way she kept all her stuff in perfect order? They should'a been with her other ones."

"So, like what are you saying?" Mariah's hands became still for the moment.

"I know this sounds far-fetched, Mariah, but what if she's still alive?"

"There's no way, we buried her, remember?"

Noah would never forget. "I overheard Uncle Cliff tell Aunt Margaret that even though he said it was Mom, he couldn't really tell 'cause of the fire. They just assumed it was her because they were pretty sure it was her car. Look, Mariah, what if she couldn't stand it anymore and felt she had to leave. You know she and Dad were fighting a lot before she died."

"She wouldn't leave us."

"We weren't always the greatest kids."

"Are you trying to make me the most miserable thirteen-year-old alive?" Mariah asked as she began to lose control of the corners of her mouth. She took up the corner of her blanket and began the repetitious fingering of its fringe that always seemed to take control of her hands whenever she sat with it. There were just a few pieces of fringe left on the blanket, and Noah had pulled it out of the cedar chest for her only that week. He didn't know if they had any more blankets like it. The last blanket had been shredded as the one before it. He kept disposing of the ruined blankets and picking up the shreds and torn lint so that his father wouldn't see them.

Later that night, instead of swallowing the white and orange capsule Noah gave her, she hid it under the scented paper her mother had lined her drawers with. Mariah had been skipping her medication as much as she could without getting caught and now there were about twenty pills hidden there. She turned out her light to go to sleep, and for the first time in many months the fantasies of her own death did not fill Mariah's mind. What if her mother *was alive*? Would Mariah answer the phone one day to hear her voice on the other end?

♦

IN ANOTHER PART of the house Mariah's father sat on the sofa in front of the television. Mason looked around the room that he and his wife had built together—he'd built the house after college, and she had hated always living in a house that was constantly under construction. For years they had had no running water. It was after Mariah was about two that his wife had packed up the children and moved out. She had been convinced that he was having an affair, but he hadn't. He doubted whether she had ever truly believed him. But she had come back saying she just couldn't go through with divorce. He had always wondered if they should have ended it then.

Mason had once watched a woman hand her lipstick to her husband as they had arrived at the front door of a restaurant. Jealously, he had watched the man slide the lipstick into his breast pocket. This was the kind of thing that had never occurred between Mason and his wife. There had never been that sense of completeness and total trust between them. As he drank one last finger of bourbon, he realized again that she had always doubted his love. He looked around the disheveled room. Although Noah did his best with the housework, there were stacks of video tapes lying here and there, and the television screen was covered with a film of dust. Mason knew he should get up and take care of the dirty glasses and plates covering the table tops and the dirty socks poking out from beneath the sofa, but he could not muster up the energy to do it.

◆

NOAH HAD BEEN SETTING HIS ALARM FOR 6 AM for several months now so that if his father were still asleep in the family room, he could get him out of there before Mariah woke up. On this morning, that is where he found his father. "Come on, Dad, get up," he said, as he shook his arm that was draped along the chair.

"What time is it?"

"Six."

"Thanks Noah," he answered. Noah watched the lean figure climb the stairs. Noah took the bourbon bottle and glass into the kitchen where he put them out of sight. The sun's light was beginning to turn the black atmosphere outside into the beginning of a day. He could see the old farmer's light across the stubble cornfield next door. He knew that the old man went to bed early and rose early too. A week didn't go by without him bringing a sweet potato pie or a casserole to Noah.

When Noah was sure that his father's shower was running, he went back to his mother's computer and opened her WordPerfect files. He first pulled up file 2468, and this is what he found:

> Dear Man Without a Pen, I was much moved by your letter and hope that my reply will be helpful. Firstly, no matter how many times your toddler steals your ball-point pens you really shouldn't get mad. Obviously, she is very upset that her daycare center wrote such severe things about her and that you then read them out loud to her grandmother on the phone. Any care provider that can't see all of God's children in a loving light should not be a care provider. All children should be told that it is their behavior that is amiss—not themselves. These are well known and practiced adages. Get her out of there! Don't kill the peony bush because it has black spot—kill the black spot. By the way, Revco is having a sale on Bic pens this week, 10 for $1. Marcelle.

Noah left the computer on as he started breakfast. Cereal for himself, oatmeal for his Dad, nothing for Mariah. Yesterday, he'd made her scrambled eggs which she hadn't touched and poptarts the day before with the same appealing effect on her. Mariah dropped her backpack on the floor beside her chair, and sat with her elbows on the table supporting her chin with her two childish hands. "You really should eat, you know." her brother said.

"I'm not hungry."

Noah watched her as he crunched his cereal. Her hair was behind her back, but she seemed a little more cheerful than usual. She actually took a bite of her poptart. "Mariah," her Dad said, "Stop fiddling with your hair." Mariah had pulled a strand of her hair forward, was twisting it around her finger, releasing it, and then starting again. She had recently twisted off much of the hair near her face so that she had begun to look a little odd.

♦

LATER THAT AFTERNOON, after getting off the school bus and walking down the graveled drive. Noah said to his sister, "I thought we could go see Mom's grave."

"How come?" she asked.

"I just think we should. It's that little voice that keeps popping into my head. I've been avoiding it for a while now, and I just think we should go."

"Well let's ride. I haven't ridden Sparkles for ages."

Noah almost said, Not since Mom died.

Mariah lead the way down across the creek because Noah's pony hated water. Sparkles steadily stepped through the moving water which came up past her knees. Noah was behind on Pickles kicking at him to make him go. Once across the creek they had to cross the state highway into the tiny hamlet of Bostwick. As Mariah listened to the rushing water behind her, she could remember the time when she was two or three and her mother had led her across the creek on Pickles. Halfway through Pickles had begun to shake like a dog shaking off water, and Mariah had ended up in the water. Her mother was laughing as she picked the toddler up and squeezed her tight. Mariah remembered that tight squeeze—she hadn't had time to cry.

The sky was gray, and the cool breeze shook the dead leaves that still clung tightly to the black branches. She watched Noah jog off at a trot. When he pulled up by the gate, he slipped down to the ground which stood only about a foot away. After going through they tied their ponies to the fence and spoke before entering the churchyard.

"How'd school go today?"

Mariah shrugged. She didn't tell him about the concerned look from her teachers at school. Since coming home from the psychiatric ward, the school had put her into the special needs program. She had only one teacher all day and was never left on her own.

"Mariah, I found these in your drawer this morning." Noah held a clear, plastic sandwich bag in his hand that contained all the orange and white capsules that she had hidden.

"So?"

"So, you're supposed to take these. I guess this means you haven't taken any of your medications?"

Mariah's lip began to tremble. "I hate taking them," she sobbed. They make me feel like hell."

Noah watched as his sister began to weep. "You have to take them. What if I'm not there to save you one of these times. It's the pills that keep you safe."

"That's a lie!"

Noah began to cry as well. "Please." his sister said. They turned away from the gate and passed into the cemetery to where their mother was buried.

The ground was covered in young green grass with small patches of the ground showing where the grass seed must not have fallen. The stone was not a rectangle but rounded at the top. An angel was engraved at the top with their mother's name beneath it. "What if she's really somewhere else?" Mariah said.

Noah didn't answer and just stood there looking at the marble headstone. He could hear Pickles shake his head from the jingle of his bit and thought about leaving. He bent down and pulled up a weed near the stone and remembered weeding with his mother, when he was just a toddler. "You're such a big boy, Noah, look at all those weeds!" she had said as he proudly pulled his wagon piled high toward the woods. But what if she wasn't really dead and was in California, somewhere, maybe where there were palm trees, sandy beaches, and the sun was always shining.

"Do you really think she's alive, Noah?" his sister asked.

What should he tell her? He wanted to say yes, but he knew he couldn't lie and that his mother had been the one found in the car crash. He was kneeling by her grave with the weed in his hand and read the inscription.

> Life is eternal,
> Not memories laid away on shelves,
> We knew her once,
> We know her still.

This was followed by his father's initials. Noah looked up at his sister who seemed to have read it at the same time. The sunlight laid patches on her head; she looked wholesome and well. Her face was still pink from their ride over, and her hands where held quietly in repose as she read the inscription. Neither one of them had seen this before because it had not been ready at the time of the funeral.

It was true, Mariah thought, her mother was still with them.

It was like the time she had picked her up from the creek and held her so tight. She could feel her now. A brightness filled her mind as she shut her eyes. She wasn't truly gone; she was still here; she had always been here. Her lilacs had bloomed fully last spring, and the mums they had planted together were presently at their height of beauty. But it wasn't just her garden; it was Noah's and her father's too. Still it wasn't just that. As the light filled her mind, she realized she couldn't lose her mother. Mariah felt as if a huge weight had been lifted from her.

Noah stood up and made his way over to Pickles. He held the gate for his sister, hopped onto his mount, and trotted after her. They rode on in silence through the red and golden fluttering leaves that floated down, shimmering, to the ground if the wind swelled too much. The sun had come out, and a rosy sunset had begun to appear on the horizon. The two ponies were jubilant as they headed for their dinner back home. After slipping down the steep hill and crossing the creek for the first time, they passed the store where Tiny opened the screen door and waved her corpulent arm at them. "Hey kids, it's a beautiful day."

"Sure is." Mariah answered as they crossed the tracks. They crossed the highway next and then forged through the same stream that Mariah had fallen into when she had been a baby. Noah came abreast of her as they came upon the dry shore.

"I'll race ya" he said. Without answering Mariah pushed her pony into a full gallop, and they were off. The two children were laughing and shouting to one another as their father drove up the gravel road. He could see them on the other side of the fence galloping toward the final ascent to their home. He pressed the accelerator to catch up.

When they realized he was there, they pushed their ponies faster to beat him. Noah was hunched forward urging Pickles on. But Mariah was sitting tall with her golden brown hair flying behind her. As their father raced them up the hill, he felt he was fourteen again trying to catch his wife who as a girl had raced him repeatedly on her pony while he struggled behind on his bike. Mariah could pass for her at this moment.

His wife must know now, he thought. She must know that he

had desired her more than anyone else in his life. He hadn't been good at saying it, but love was at the center of his being for her. His daughter's face caught his attention—she was looking at him as she glanced back in her race for home. Their eyes caught each other, and he knew she was again the child he had lost.

She tossed her head forward and tore in front of the car's path to get to the barn. He had to touch the brakes to give her enough berth. Noah followed close at her heels as they sped around the corner and out of sight.

When they came in from the barn, Mason was mopping the kitchen floor. "Don't come in that door!" he hollered. That's just what their mother would have said. They walked around to the front door and were met with the smell of biscuits baking in the oven. "I guess she taught him how to bake too. " Noah said.

"I guess so." His sister answered as she sat down at her mother's computer. "I know she has a recipe for peach cobbler in here somewhere. I don't know if I ever told you or not, but Mom and I organized all of her files together one day. I can find anything you need in here."

Israel Rea is a writer and businessman in Atlanta.

KATE CHENEY CHAPPELL

Return to the Summer House

I

Air before rain,
air so sweet
I weep
my grandmother's tears
as I open
each window
        of the closed house,
remembering the scent of water
in the air,
and her hair down to brush out
before the sun had fully set,
that slow, slow going down of the July day,
the smell of gas from the stove
where she was warming milk
    to drink before bed.
How fresh the sheets of night air
    that surround a child of eight,
how close the sound of the whip-poor-will
at dusk,
    how certain the smell of her
grandmother's old skin.

II

When we got to the cottage, the grass was not
    mowed.
It lay like long bleached hair
in swirls
    as if underwater,
flattened like beds where lovers had lain.
I feel their ghosts as close as the marks
left by damp hair against damp skin,
like corn husk where the silk has pressed,
like rivulets of sand where the tide has run.

III

I shiver
walking naked to the bathroom,
the night sky follows me at every window,
last streaks of sun linger on the horizon
after the storm has passed,
the sky above
    still,
        black on blue,
and the flames of light lick out
like tongues on the rim of the sea.
Returning, I sleep the deep
sleep of the very young who go to bed
before the sun.

Kate Cheney Chappell has worked primarily in watercolor for the past fifteen years, and has had numerous one-person shows in New England, including three at Harvard Divinity School. One of her watercolors was featured on the cover of *Chrysalis* (Spring 1993).

Enamels—Champlevé. Crosier head, with St. Michael fighting the devil. Champlevé enamel on gilt copper, ca. 1200. The crosier was often buried with the bishop who had carried it; many examples from the Limoges area are known from c. 1165–1250. New York: The Metropolitan Museum of Art. The Friedsam Collection, Bequest of Michael Friedsam, 1931.

♦ **MICHAEL D. PHILLIPS** ♦

The Problem with Evil

♦

"He[1] is almighty, isn't He? He could use His might to save the victims, but He doesn't! So—on whose side is He? Could the killer kill without his blessing—without his complicity?"

—Ellie Wiesel, *The Trial of God*

THE EXISTENCE OF EVIL is the perennial problem in the fabric of a universe understood to be *creatio ex nihilo,* i.e. created from nothing by an all powerful, perfectly good God. The difficulty stems from the logical inconsistency in holding that (1) God is all powerful; (2) God is perfectly good; and (3) Evil exists. To believe any two negates the third. The existence of evil inevitably raises questions about faith and trust in a God who would permit it.

When faith communities address the problem of evil, they tend to develop theodicies (arguments validating God's goodness and justice despite evil's existence). A diversity of theodicies exist, even within the same communities. Examining Classical Christianity (Calvin's *Institutes*), Jewish mysticism (Kabbalah), and Process Theology (A. N. Whitehead's theories as developed by Dr. Charles Hartshorne and others) provide us with an opportunity to weigh the place of evil in the universe.

Calvin held in his *Institutes* that there is no place in human affairs for fortune and chance.[2] All that occurs rests within the providential decree of God. Even Adam's original sin was decreed by God, yet Adam remains accountable (guilty as charged). Our human inability to comprehend God's intentions in utilizing evil in the divine plan of redemption is not just or sufficient cause to charge God with complicity in the advent of evil, according to Calvin. Central to Calvin's theory is that no one is innocent, and all merit destruction, yet, by God's election of grace, a few are spared.

Calvin's intention, it must be stated, was pastoral. He hoped to provide a vision of redemption transcending the evil of this world, concluding that God is finally in charge and ever shall be.

Kabbalist teachings (a form of Jewish mysticism) are obscure paradoxes contemplated by its adherents and represent a revolt against the Jewish and Christian (anti-mythical) philosophies of the Middle Ages. In the Kabbalah, God can only be understood by means of ten Sefiroth (potencies of God), which are external emanations of His creative power and life. These manifested potencies of God appear collectively and harmoniously, yet also have inherent polar elements that are the source of apparent conflict. So long as they are contemplated together, harmony and balance are maintained. But when contemplated divisively, discord is the result.

One tension point in Kabbalist teachings involves the Sefirah *Hesed* (freely flowing, freely given good of divine love, grace, and charity) and the Sefirah *Gevurah* (severity, judgment, self-containment, and, therefore, restrictive power). The tale of Adam's sin was expressed by the earliest Spanish Kabbalists within a passage known as "The Secret of the Tree of Knowledge." A pre-eminent scholar of the Kabbalah, Gershom Scholem, interprets this passage (an allegory of the Garden of Eden) as follows:

> Man's two urges or drives, for good and for evil, are implanted within him as possibilities of action, just as the qualities of love and severity are present in God. Had Adam subordinated his will to that of God, in which all contradictions function in sacred harmony, then the restrictive factor within himself, the Evil Urge, would have been nullified within the totality of his being, and evil would never have emerged as a reality, but remained as potential. But Adam . . . by his improper contemplation of the Divine, caused a separation within the Godhead [with] a baleful effect on . . . Creation.

Evil is not explained away by God's ultimate just rule making it irrelevant (Calvin). Rather in Kabbalism evil is a potential but not a necessary modality. When all things are viewed as a whole, God's creation is fundamentally good. In isolation, however, certain elements can be destructive. There is no real dichotomy between good and evil because both have originated from God. A shortcoming of the Kabbalist doctrine, however, is that the Holy God withdraws from participation in the world following the advent of real evil.

Scripture can be read to represent both Calvin and Kabbalist views. In the Tanakh (the Jewish Bible), evil is represented as part and parcel of God's original Creation:

> That they may know from the rising of the sun, and from the west, that there is none beside me. I am the Lord, and there is none else. I form the light, and create darkness: I make peace, and create evil: I the Lord do all these things." (Isaiah 45$^{5-6}$)

> The Lord hath made every thing for His own purpose, Yea, even the wicked for the day of evil. (Proverbs 16:4)

Still, the creation account declares "God saw that it was very good" (Genesis 1:31).

According to Gershom Scholem, the Bible's "unequivocal attitude [regarding evil's origins with God] was clouded by the intrusion of Greek speculation into the world of monotheistic religions. The opposites of light and darkness, good and evil, spirit and matter, take on a completely different meaning in Platonic thought than they do in the ancient texts."[4] Historical shifts in metaphysical constructs have led to new interpretations of ancient understandings, often in response to circumstances of crisis. Precipitating events in Jewish history were the Babylonian Exile, circa 580 BCE, and the Maccabean Revolt, circa 160 BCE. A similar crisis in Christian (and Jewish) history was the crucifixion of Rabbi Yeshua Ha Notsri (Jesus of Nazareth), circa 30 CE. At some such juncture, the separation of good and evil was cast as absolute. God (Spirit) was understood to be good, and the world (flesh/matter) was fundamentally evil.

The insight of Process Theology is to posit that contraries need not necessarily be contradictories. For instance, God can be both absolute and relative. **That God is** (God's existence) and **Who God is** (God's nature) are absolutes in God's person. **What God is** remains relative, since God is constantly in the process of becoming (I will be who I will be, Exodus 3:14). God is absolutely ultimate—unsurpassed and unsurpassable. Yet, God is able to surpass God's self from moment to moment (hence, God is also relative). God's relationship to the universe is simultaneously transcendent and immanent. God is not simply the universe (Pantheism) nor separate from the universe (Deism and some strains of Classical

Theism). Rather, God is both Immanent in the universe and transcendent of the universe; He is truly "with us" (and all of creation).

The problem with evil is resolved by attenuating the claim that God is omnipotent (all powerful). To say that God has all power is to negate the very real experience that each of us has in exercising at least some power in bringing about changes in our lives or in the pursuit of our interests. If you and I do exercise some power, then evil is a possible corollary in that participation. In Process Theory God remains the most powerful, but not the only power. This difference is a critical one. While an all powerful God bears with evil, allowing it but not subject to it, a God of relative (finite) power bears evil, i.e., suffers the torments of evil. This God is indeed a "God with us." Could the same be said of Calvin's or Kabbalist teachings? No, since the all powerful God of Calvin fails to act against evil in order to fulfill the divine plan, and the all powerful God of the Kabbalah withdraws God's self from the existence of evil to preserve holiness. Only the God of Process Theology embraces a suffering world, since God is that single actual entity (person) perfectly related to all other actual entities (persons in the broadest sense).

Another important distinction in Process Theology versus Classical and Kabbalist theologies is the kind of power that God exercises. The God of Calvin exercises a coercive power, i.e., we will inevitably do what God has decreed, and we have no real power to alter this. The God of the Kabbalah appears indifferent in this respect, having withdrawn from any active participation in creation because evil has erupted here (Adam's sin). The God of Process Theology exercises persuasive power. God respects the freedom of every other actual entity. God does not choose to exercise power persuasively, rather, this is the only form of power available to a God who is both immanent (within the universe), and transcendent (surpassing the universe), and not absolute (apart from the universe).

Hartshorne describes God's exercise of power in terms analogous to how a brain (the mental pole) works with a body (the physical pole) in order to accomplish various tasks. The individual cells are not commanded directly (coerced) by the brain, nor can they be. The brain instead provides an overarching stimulus that directs (persuasively) the activity of the body in accordance with needs common to both brain and body. The individual cells retain a degree of autonomy. The cells can both feel and decide for their own interests. These interests may or may not coincide with the greater interests of the body (as perceived by the brain) from moment to moment. Cells can even rebel, becoming cancerous, destroying the body. The brain (God) cannot guarantee total harmony. The brain (God) strives to optimize harmony as best as can be done given the ongoing (autonomous) activities of distinct and separate cells carrying out (simultaneously) life processes important to them as well as to the body.

Hartshorne draws heavily upon Plato for his metaphysic. An argument of Plato's from Book Ten of the *Laws* can be summarized:

> (1) Psychical process or soul is the only self-explanatory process, the only self-determining type of change; (2) Order among souls, and hence in reality generally, can be explained only through a supremely good soul, which persuades the others to conform to its decisions; and (3) Disorder and evil are not due to the supreme soul's decisions, but to the conflicting decisions of other souls.[5]

But Hartshorne disagrees with Plato's synonymous use of the terms 'disorder' and 'evil'. Both order and disorder (chaos) are positive principles. In a marvelous paragraph Hartshorne states it like this:

> Order is the limit imposed upon chaos. It is not the alternative to or the absence of chaos, but its qualification as limited or partial, rather than absolute or pure chaos. Order is just the limiting of chaos, as a river is the channeling (not the absence) of water.[6]

God, then has a will for creation that optimizes the freedom and creativity of every actual entity (including God). Sin is our tendency to resist God's persuasive challenge toward the good of all. Evil results when we implement sinful desires to the harm of others (and the God who is perfectly related to them). Here is the true strength of this metaphysic—its insistence that we (the free agents) are responsible, collectively, for the world as it is, and for the world that is coming into being. We are responsible both for the evil that we do and that which we allow. By doing or allowing evil, we fail: (1) to love God with all the heart, soul, mind, and strength; (2) to love the neighbor as ourselves; and (3) to love ourselves because we perpetrate harm against the One most perfectly related to us—God! It is by God's design that we each participate in the universe freely and creatively, moment to moment. God is the supreme example of free and creative activity within this universe in accordance with both the promise and the command of love, and for this reason is supremely worthy of worship for having transcended self-interest, granting both life and liberty to all others.

Further, God is not immune to this world's suffering (the evil that we do), but He is with us, that is, God is a fellow sufferer. Because the person of God is perfectly related to every other person, God feels the immediacy of all our suffering. At the same time, God feels the satisfaction of those who have caused our suffering for their own selfish interests. But, since God is necessarily ethical, it would be impossible for Him to experience the satisfaction of those who pursue evil without His own torment. Since God is perfectly related to all of creation, God experiences both the agony of the tormented and the satisfaction of the tormentors, and (being ethical) God is tormented by both experiences. Is it any wonder that such a God (a God who is perfectly related to all others and necessarily ethical) would command the world to love God with all the heart, soul, mind, and strength and to love our neighbors as ourselves?

Mike Phillips is the Director of Christian Education at First Presbyterian Church, Shelbyville, Indiana, and a senior student at Christian Theological Seminary, Indianapolis. He volunteers as a minister to victims of HIV+/AIDS in Indianapolis, and struggles (with many others) to make sense of faith in a world filled with the complementary poles of joy and tragedy, commingled and inseparable.

Notes

1. I apologize for the gender language used for God throughout by quoted sources, retained 'as is'. These should be viewed as metaphorical representations of God, in accordance with the understandings of the various authors, but not necessarily representative of God's actual self.
2. McNeill, John T., ed. *Calvin: Institutes of the Christian Religion*. Philadelphia: The Westminster Press, 1960. p. 1660.
3. Scholem, Gershom. *On the Mystical Shape of the Godhead: Basic Concepts in the Kabbalah*. New York: Schocken Books, 1991. pp. 69–71.
4. *Ibid*, p.57.
5. Dombrowski, Daniel A. Hartshorne and Plato. In *The Philosophy of Charles Hartshorne*, edited by Lewis Edwin Hahn. La Salle: Open Court, 1991. p. 483.
6. Hartshorne, Charles. *Philosophers Speak of God*. University of Chicago Press, 1953. p. 436.

♦ SONIA SHAH ♦

To Live the Faith

♦

I CAME TO THE PARK to see an old friend. I was in search of answers to the riddle of faith. I thought that I had long ago discarded the rituals of religion. My God had become independence, not servitude, freedom not obedience, action not contemplation. My life had been full of excitement, turmoil, and accomplishments, and I loved it. So what was I searching for, and why had I found myself lighting a candle for my mother while on a tour of the cathedral last week? More importantly, why had it pleased me so much? My childhood friend was waiting for me, perhaps to answer that question.

Nawar wore a peach-colored, cotton *silwar khamiz,* Pakistani clothing that consisted of baggy pants and a long overdress. I could not see her hair under the long scarf called a *dhuparta,* but I knew it was the color of a shiny new penny. Nawar sat next to me on the bench, her eyes watching her son as his sturdy, three-year-old legs carried him to the swings. "I no longer have to 'think the trivia'," she said. "Most of the tedious decisions are easy because my religion has already decided for me." We had grown up together in a small Ohio town, when her name was still Judy Jackson. She had left Ohio for Boston armed with a brand-new law degree and the determination to make a name for herself. I couldn't believe she could be saying that she didn't want to make her own decisions or think for herself. I waited for her to explain.

"I know you're thinking that I've become a mindless ninny and that I blindly follow a religion without question. It's not true. I admit there are restrictions on what I do and wear, but I feel more freedom than I ever have before. I'm free to think in a way that is more meaningful and exciting."

Finn, Voss. Computer-generated illustration in Adobe Illustrator, 1995.

"Don't Muslim women have to be obedient to their husbands? Jeez, Judy, you're an attorney. How could you give up your rights?"

"What rights? The right to be treated like a second-class citizen by the male attorneys in my office? To be judged by how I look, how I dress, or how fast I can come up with a snappy comeback to a come-on? I came to the law firm so full of ideals." She looked away wistfully as though she could see the young attorney she had been. "I started out doing the tedious work of the office, the stuff the real attorneys didn't want to do. It was okay, I expected it. I chose my clothes, my hobbies, my makeup, my car, and my address with my career in mind. All my decisions had to be weighed carefully. Should I be friendly, aloof, professional, bossy, or subservient to this client or that law partner? I was tense and very nervous. My self-esteem got beaten up. From one moment to the next, I never knew exactly what to do." She leaned toward me, the tension in her body describing her anguish. "Every decision had ramifications that could spell the end of my career. My husband, Ahmad, actually has less control over me now than my boss did then. He seldom tells me what to do, and I certainly don't feel as though I can't voice an opinion that is different from his."

"Judy, what you are talking about is just office politics. Don't you think you would have gotten used to it?"

"Perhaps. But at what price? As far as the firm was concerned, I made a mistake when I married Ahmad because he didn't suit the image of the group. I realized then that I could never be the kind of attorney this organization or any other expected. I felt that I would never know the rules because the rules kept changing, and, more importantly, I would never belong. As a Muslim sister, I know the rules, and knowing them makes all my decisions and interactions smooth and stress-free. It is very exciting."

"Exciting?" Now I was really confused. When we were growing up, Judy seldom followed the rules and always came up with exciting schemes. She usually got us into trouble. I remembered Judy standing next to me in front of the classroom, our heads down. I was scared and unwilling to look Miss Jones in the eye. Judy had her head down so Miss Jones wouldn't realize that she was trying to control her laughter. The Home Economics teacher was a fussy little woman who wore glasses and spent half of every class looking for them. It was Judy who decided to drop them in the banana-bread batter. It really was pretty funny when the glasses were pried out of the gooey cake. What had happened to that Judy?

"What are these rules that are so exciting to you?" I asked.

"Well, I rise before sunup and begin my day by preparing for my prayers. Muslims must be very clean when praying, in fact, our prayers really begin when we wash ourselves. There is a very precise way of doing this ritual. My first prayer of the day is offered before sunrise. I take great care to say prayers correctly in Arabic, and I face toward Mecca. Covering my head and neck, I wear clothes that assure that nothing is exposed except my hands, bare feet, and face. Repeating these prayers five times throughout the day, I am a much better person. How can one have petty or unkind thoughts when prayers are sprinkled throughout the day? How could I become angry or upset with the circumstances of my life when every day I am giving thanks for that life?"

"Do you always wear that thing on your head?" I asked.

She smiled and said, "I wear it whenever I expect to leave the house or if men other than close family come to visit. It's hard to explain, but my entire being changes when I put on the head covering. It is like a mantle of protection and a barrier between me and the things of the world that bring anxiety and stress. I walk differently. I talk differently. I keep my eyes averted from men and my thoughts clean. Many modern Muslim women do not wear the traditional clothing, but because I do I am instantly accepted and made to feel at ease. These clothes set me apart, when I'm on the street. I feel surrounded by serenity and peace."

♦

THE AMISH ORDER AND ISLAM may seem far apart in perspective, but the similarities are many. They both have a dress code and strict rules that guide everyday lives.

Another friend, Rachel, and I had played together as small children during summers spent at my aunt's farm. We always met at the edge of the cornfield. We both walked barefoot, but that's where the resemblance ended. I had on well-worn shorts and a shirt. She wore a dress of brown cotton with a black apron over it and a starched white muslin cap with its ties hanging down loosely. I looked like a ragamuffin, and she looked like a miniature adult. I had a doll with rubber arms that said mama when I turned her over, and she had one dressed just like herself, but it had no face. She said dolls were not supposed to have faces. She let me play with her doll but would never touch mine. We generally had a good time, but she had a disconcerting way of falling silent and calmly looking at me whenever I did something mischievous, such as trying out a new swear word on everyone I knew. My aunt was shocked, my mother washed my mouth out, and my dad gave me a sharp whack on the back of my head for swearing, but it was Rachel's patient stare without comment that made me decide to find another way to express myself. Now, twenty years later, my talk with Judy brought Rachel to mind. The picture I saw was the moment she had stared at me, without a word. Her disapproving look conveyed a more powerful message to me than any chastening words or corrective actions from my parents.

I visited Rachel, when back in Ohio. Holding a glass of cool apple cider, I sat in her well-kept, orderly kitchen and noticed the pump on the sink and kerosene lanterns. When we finished catching up on our lives, I told her about Judy, now known as Nawar, and the peace of mind she had found.

Rachel said, "I can't talk about finding peace and serenity because this is the only life I have ever known; and as you know, one of the basics of the Amish Order is to keep apart from the rest of the world. Our life within the community is rich, full, and orderly. It has a rhythm that is calm and sweet. There's a certainty that all will be as it should be. Pain and trouble come to us all, but there is comfort in knowing that I am safe from some things. I will never have a husband who beats me because violence is forbidden. I will never go hungry or be without shelter because the Amish take care of each other. The worst thing that could happen would be to be shunned."

"What would happen?" I asked.

"If a member of the Order does something against our teaching, that person may be shunned. A shunned person can't come to services; no one speaks to him, does business with him, or has anything to do with him or his family. The shunned person must eat alone, and, if it is a man, he must prepare his own meals because his wife cannot. It is a terrible thing.

I am also in no danger of having my pride wounded. Care has been taken to eliminate those things that encourage pride."

"For instance?"

"After Sunday service we share a meal. It's prepared by the person at the house where the service is held. The food is always made the same way—beans, bread, and apple pie. The women don't try to outdo each other."

"Is that why you all dress alike?"

"That's one reason. When I get dressed to go to church or to visit a friend, I can't say, 'Oh, what shall I wear? What's the prettiest thing I have? I want everyone to notice me.' My clothes look the same as every other Amish woman's. Our plain dress sets us apart from the world. We know where we belong and that we belong where we are."

◆

BELONGING TO SOMETHING GRAND while at the same time being separate answers a need for Rachel but not for all others. My neighbor Jenny has tried to be a "good Orthodox Jewish wife." Her own family observed most of the holidays but had a casual attitude about ritual and tradition. When Jenny married, she determined to follow her husband Samuel's lead and do everything correctly. She learned all the rules and carefully followed them. She looked at me with wounded eyes and said, "I try and I try, but it just doesn't work. When we were first married, our families thought we made a terrible mistake. Now my mother-in-law brags to all her friends that I keep perfect kosher, know all the prayers, dress right, and never make mistakes. I get wonderful approval which makes Samuel so proud. He thinks we have proven them wrong, but the truth is I'm just going though the motions. I believe with all my heart that this is the best way to live, but it's like wearing someone else's skin. Now I am so different from my own family that I don't belong there either."

♦

FOUR CHILDHOOD FRIENDS live their different faiths. One friend stands at a mirror and dons a long cloth, wrapping it securely around her head and neck. This commonplace action she is transports her to a feeling of strength and joy. The Amish friend continues on a path she has always known, finding comfort in simplicity and order. The third friend finds ritual meaningless and feels resentment and emptiness.

Alauddin Attar, a Sufi master, said, "All religion is something other than what it is assumed to be. Religion is a vehicle. Its expression, rituals, morals, and teachings are designed to cause certain elevating effects, at a certain time, upon certain groups."

Lighting the candle for my mother rekindled the flame of my childhood beliefs. I can see better where I am going when I understand from whence I have come. In offering a prayer in the cathedral, I lit a candle to keep my mother in mind, but I was also lighting a candle for my independence, for my exploration of life on my own terms. To live the faith, you have to have faith in yourself.

Sonia Shah, who lives and works in Massachusetts, is the Equal Opportunity Officer for Boston University, the president of Equal-Voice Publishing in Brookline, and senior consultant for Diversity and Management Associates, Inc., in Roxbury.

JUDITH DOHERTY QUANN

Molten Transformations

Holy water, sweet like honey,
pews of polished wood,
dripping wax from ivory candles,
gilded starburst encasing You.

Church of my childhood,
in pleated plaid, I knelt,
then stood and sang to grinding ring
of organ pipes, praying twice.

Through glass patchwork,
sunlight streams were triangles of you
reaching toward me. I basked
and bowed to Presence.

Three decades pass.

Church of my childhood,
click of heels on wood flooring,
multitudes sing a recessional hymn,
process away, from black-suited men.

In search of music, seekers risk
paths of doubt, terrain that fatigues.
From steeples, into fields of goldenrod
they still look for you, Grace.

Stream of holy water at river's edge,
resting place on the branch of a tree,
glow of lantern penetrates night,
stars burst, altered images of the Divine.

Judith Doherty Quann teaches adult education and was awarded a 1994 fellowship with the Boston Writing Project.

PART III
Heavenly Secrets

◆

The heavenly level
is opened
by a celestial love of uses,
which is a love
for the Divine.

—ADAPTED FROM SWEDENBORG

♦ BECKY CONDIT ♦

Indian Creation Stories

♦

Shasta
How Old Man Above Created the World

WHEN THE WORLD was so new that even the Stars were dark, it was very, very flat.

The Old Man above could not see through the dark. He could not step down to it because it was so far below him. With a large stone he bored a hole in Sky. Through the hole he pushed down Snow and Ice. A great pyramid was formed, and Old Man Above climbed down through the hole.

The Sun shone through the hole in the Sky and melted the Ice and Snow. The Birds and Animals were formed as he saw fit. When the foreigners came to our Country, Old Man Above went away.

Dieguenos
The Story of Creation

WHEN THE MAKER OF THE WORLD made all things, the Earth was the Woman, and the Sky was the Man. The world at this time was covered with a pure lake of water.

The Maker took tobacco in his hands, rubbed it fine, and blew upon it three times. Everytime he blew, the heavens rose higher above their heads.

This was done several times until the sky was so high it formed a concave arch.

Untitled Painting depicting the Navaho legend of the creation of the Milky Way. Shown are two yei figures asleep beneath a tree while Coyote throws the stars haphazardly into the sky. The task of placing the stars and constellations in the sky was given to several individuals. Displeased that he had not been asked and impatient at the slow speed at which the task was being done, Coyote mischievously stole the stars which had not yet been placed and tossed them into the sky, where they remained (artist unknown, 1965–1975, Navajo Indian Reservation, Window Rock, Arizona).

Then they faced North, South, East, and West. After this he dug a hole in the ground and found mud. This is what he made the first Indian out of.

He dug another hole to make man and after that a woman. He made man very easy. Woman was harder to make. All other things followed as needed. When the Maker completed all of this, he Created nothing more.

Eskimo
The Origin of Sun, Moon and Stars

AT A TIME WHEN DARKNESS covered the Earth, a girl was nightly visited by someone whose identity she could not discover. She found out that it was her brother. The father and mother were very angry. The son ran away. The daughter took a brand from the fire and ran after him. He ran to the Sky to get away. The Man changed into the Moon, and the girl became the Sun. The Sparks that flew from the Brand became the Stars.

Pit River Story
The Creation of Mankind

SILVER FOX AND COYOTE lived together. Silver Fox gathered some Service Berry sticks and whittled them down. Working all night, the shavings were to be made into Common People. The finished sticks were to be warriors and chiefs.

Yuchi
In the Beginning

SOUTHEASTERN INDIAN *traditions believe in an Upper World, a Lower World, and This World, where they, the animals, and plants lived and thrived.*

Early on in This World, some special humans and animals came down to visit from Upper World.

Humans of this World learned to make and maintain order between themselves and the other two Worlds.

They became mostly villagers and agriculturists with more permanent tribal homes, since they were not nomadic by nature. Their tribes enlarged and prospered as hunters, fisherman, builders, and skilled craftsman, including the women's abilities in weaving, basketry, and herbal medicines; the latter maintaining the good health of their people in mind, body, and spirit.

Makah
When the Animals and Birds Were Created

WHEN THE WORLD was very young, there were no people on the earth. There were no birds or animals either.

There was nothing but grass and sand and creatures. They were neither animal nor people but had some of the traits of people and some of animals.

The two brothers of the Sun and the Moon came to the earth. They came to make the earth ready for a new race of people, the Indians. The two called all Creatures to them. Some were changed to animals and birds. Some they changed to trees and smaller plants.

Becky Condit is a descendent of Chief John Ross, Principal Chief of the Cherokee Nation during the time of the "Trail of Tears." Her Grandmother and Grandfather recounted stories to her as a child, and they told her to remember her people whence she came. Becky has written several books on Indian myths and legends. Her stories are created within the context of nature's harmony and her own belief in the continuity of spiritual descent from generations past. This belief is often symbolized by the circle or hoop of life, a common element in many Native American stories.

Panel from a dado of a building. Nishapur, Iran, carved stucco, originally painted, tenth century. Nishapur was a center for learning. The New York: Metropolitan Museum of Art. Excavations of 1936 and Rogers Fund, 1937.

♦ *WILSON VAN DUSEN* ♦

The Cosmic Order

♦

IT IS FORTUNATE that we seem to be in such an ordered universe that the physical laws that apply here seem to apply throughout space. It is cheering to our struggling understanding to be greeted by this consistency of order, yet our understanding is very uneven. We can achieve precision in measures at both the atomic and the astronomical level, but our understanding of our personal psycho-physical order is far from clear. I warrant that we could stare at a perfect depiction of the order of all things and not recognize it.

The eighteenth-century scientist Emanuel Swedenborg (1666–1772) came back from decades of spiritual exploration and reported just such a comprehensive order. His description of the cosmic order is so perfect and consistent that it shows throughout all thirty volumes of his spiritual findings. Swedenborg sprinkled descriptions of events in the spiritual world like marginal field notes among his straightforward accounts.

On one of Swedenborg's spiritual journeys to a lower spiritual world, he was challenged by a demon to describe the cosmic order. Swedenborg's tone is a bit impatient because he knows the demon's disposition is against order. The demon said, "Are you the man who thinks and speaks about order? Tell me briefly what order is." I give this account because it is a wonderful summary.

> To this I replied: "I will tell you the general principles, but not particulars, because you cannot understand them," and I proceeded to enumerate them as follows: (1) God is order itself. (2) He created man from order, in order, and for order. (3) He created man's rational mind according to the order of the whole spiritual world, and his body according to the order of the whole natural world. On this account man was called by the Ancients a heaven in little, and a world in little. (4) Therefore it is a law of order that a man from his own little heaven or little spiritual world should govern his own microcosm or little

natural world, just as God from His great heaven or spiritual world governs the macrocosm or natural world in all things in general and in particular. (5) It is a consequent law of order that a man ought to enter into faith by truths from the Word and into charity by good works, and so reform and regenerate himself. (6) It is a law of order that a man should purify himself from sins by his own labor and power, and not stand still believing in his own impotency, and expecting God forthwith to wash away his sins. (7) It is a further law of order that a man should love God with all his soul and with all his heart, and his neighbor as himself, and not wait in the expectation that these loves will be put into his mind and heart in an instant by God, just as bread from the baker's is put into his mouth. And there are many more laws like these.

—*True Christian Religion*, Paragraph 71

There is so much condensed here. God is order itself. This is so true, he says elsewhere, that even God cannot act against this order because to do so would be contrary to His nature. He created man (and all things) in this order. Elsewhere Swedenborg says even man's body reflects the order of the natural world. We are created for order in the sense that we are part of the forces that create order.

His third point that our mind was created to reflect the order of the spiritual world needs a bit of elaboration. In the hierarchy of existence there is in sequence the Lord, the celestial, the spiritual, our rational, our senses, and the natural world. We are a heaven (and also a church) in the least form in that the structure of all the spiritual is mirrored in our mind within.* We are most aware of our rational and sensory (our most limited aspects), but we can become aware of our higher and normally less conscious aspects.

In his points 4 to 7, Swedenborg states an essential paradox. It is as though we are ruler in our own world, and we are to rule it as well as we can. We are not to act like baby birds waiting for someone to put food into our mouths. But if we reflect on all our efforts, we come to see that we are simply a part of order, and that order is assisting us. We are to do as well as we can, but knowing full well we are assisted by the order we did not create and barely

---

*Swedenborg's spiritual experience led him to rediscover the ancient idea of humans as a microcosm that accurately reflects the macrocosm, or the total of reality. So a person can be a heaven in the least form (*Divine Love and Wisdom*, paragraphs 319 to 323), and similarly the good person is a church in the least form (*Arcana Coelestia* [*Heavenly Secrets*], paragraphs 82e and 6113).

understand. So we are created *from order,* and put *in order,* that we might be *for order.* Swedenborg also speaks extensively of uses in which we act *for order.* The preceding gives a kind of hierarchical order in which the Lord steps down through successive and discrete levels from the celestial, to the spiritual, to our rational. And this stepping down has everything to do with how our minds (which are a heaven in the least form) operate.

Swedenborg further describes a kind of willfulness that operates through all levels of creation. The *end* finds a *cause* that enables it to create *an effect.* He stresses that only in all three is there existence. Ends which do not find a cause and create an effect are as nothing. Again the formula is the same for the individual as it is on a cosmic level. What we really love, which is our end, seeks out a means (a cause) to eventually realize itself in an effect. If, for example, the goal is to love your son or daughter, one way to love her is to listen (cause), the result being that she feels heard or loved (effect) and becomes the loved daughter (end). The love, or affective aspect of ourselves is partly known to us and partly not known.

Swedenborg also describes this same willfulness on a cosmic level. God is End itself. God created humans that they may come into conjunction with God. Elsewhere Swedenborg says the aim of creation is that there be a heaven on earth, that is, a heavenly influx for the human race. Thus, the One works through all creation so that its creation might return to its Source.

There is another and rather practical way of looking at this cosmic order. If we understand the order in which we are embedded, we can better work with it. If we choose to participate in order and for order, we become part of the order itself. Right action puts us in order that we might be *for order.* This is the key to opening the higher aspects of the heaven in the least form which we are. As we understand and try to cooperate with order, we become "in the image of God" which is order itself. It also means we come into fundamental touch with our own ordered nature.

A long-term scholar of mysticism and comparative religions, **Dr. Van Dusen** is currently at work on a book that summarizes the experience of God across many major religions.

NAOMI GLADISH SMITH

Bryonia, Belladonna, and My Father

♦

THERE'S A LOT TO BE SAID FOR ORDER. Especially in a child's life. Our family had its share of stresses, its share of disruptions and heartbreak, but as I look back on my childhood, I realize that there was a sense of order, a sense that no matter what might darken the world, my parents, and in one respect especially my father, would hold chaos at bay. I know now that this was a result of his deeply held religious beliefs, but the image that represented this sense of order and security to me as a young child was an old shoe box filled with neatly arranged little bottles of homeopathic medicine.

Homeopathy was about as close as my father came to having a hobby. Of course, he shouldn't have dispensed medicines any more than an amateur aficionado of traditional medicine should share his favorite pills and remedies, but my father only attempted to alleviate minor, commonplace ills. For the serious stuff, he consulted his brother, an M.D. and a homeopathic physician. But because our family was usually in a town, a state, or a country away from my uncle's office, this often had to be done by phone or letter.

My father's shoe box was crammed with little bottles, some brown and some clear glass, some stoutly square, some slim and cylindrical, and all neatly ordered in alphabetical rows from *Aconite* to *Zincum Metallicum*. Some contained flat topped, powdery tasting globules; these were my least favorite. Some held grains so tiny they seemed like sugar-coated sand, and some, my favorites, were little sugar pellets. All smelled and tasted deliciously of alcohol.

"Stick out your tongue," my father would say as I'd tilt back my head to receive the medicine.

McCarthy, Dian. *Homeopathic Remedies*. Pencil, 1994.

"Don't chew them, let them dissolve," he'd warn me.

I wouldn't have thought of it. I sucked the sweet, alcohol-tinged pellets as slowly as I could, savoring the familiar, comforting taste as the cool liquid slid down my throat.

As a child, I wasn't often sick, and although I didn't actually look forward to a bout in bed, illness had its compensations, for then I was the focus of my father's attention. I never knew him as the bright theological graduate sent to England or as the youngest priest ever to have been ordained into the second degree of the ministry of the Swedenborgian Church. My memories are of the man he became after the motorcycle accident that left him in a coma for twelve days. My mother recounts that when four months pregnant with me, she sat by his hospital bed for those twelve long days until on the twelfth day he awoke and promptly ordered himself from the hospital, taking up his parish duties as though the accident had been a minor indisposition. From that time on and ever after, however, things were different. My father found it difficult to concentrate. When he was typing or even writing by hand, there sometimes seemed to be a block between mind and fingers. He would miss the proper typewriter keys by a hair's breadth; the hand holding the pen would wave agonizingly over the paper as though it refused to accept the message given by his brain.

Just before the outbreak of World War II, our family returned from a twelve-year stay in England. Appointed to a small, far-flung congregation near Cincinnati, my father tried desperately to carry out his duties, despite his incomplete recovery from the accident, an ill, again-pregnant wife, and five children who had come down with everything from measles to chicken pox. During those months, however, no matter how tired or harried he might be, when one of us succumbed to the current epidemic, my father gave the sufferer his full attention. He'd ask those arcane homeopathic questions: "Does it hurt in the front part of your head or further back? Does your throat tickle or does it hurt when you cough?"

Then he'd go off to study his books and come up with a remedy of something that, given once every three hours for three doses, was expected to bring relief. And it usually did.

Despite all his problems, or perhaps because of them, when we returned from England, he chose to do battle with the public school system over homeopathic vaccination. Though the elder children hadn't the scars that usually indicate a smallpox vaccination, the school accepted without question that the elder children had been inoculated. Even the stickiest of school authorities realized it wasn't possible to get school records out of an England fighting for her life. (I don't think my parents offered the fact that these inoculations were homeopathic.) I, however, five years old and entering kindergarten, had to produce evidence that I'd been vaccinated.

I don't know why my parents and the school chose to carry on their battle by means of politely worded letters, but I do know that when I brought the third or fourth note to the school nurse insisting I'd had a homeopathic vaccination, she took me to an exasperated gentleman, some sort of school official. Why he would have felt it necessary to discuss homeopathy with a five year old, I can't imagine, but he did. I answered his questions as best I could, told him that Mummy and Daddy had sent away for my Uncle Don's medicine and that I'd taken it. I forget whether I told him how good it tasted.

"It won't do," this august personage said. "It won't do at all."

But it did. Though I don't quite know how he managed it, my father prevailed, and I never did have the regular smallpox vaccination. It was a small victory, perhaps the only one my father had in that sad, strange year, a year that ended in his leaving the ministry and taking the family into the Illinois countryside where he made bombs in a nearby arsenal.

The little bottles of homeopathic medicines came with us, however, and after the war when my father found work in a Chicago laboratory assaying metals, the neatly arranged shoe box was taken along and carefully lodged in my parents' bureau drawer. I remember watching my father's blackened, burned fingers as he carefully folded a piece of paper and measured a minuscule heap of tiny granules into it. His fine, scholar's hands, ravaged by the acids and chemicals used to assay metals, sometimes shook as he gently tapped the bottle. It may have been fatigue that caused the tremor—exhaustion from night shifts—or it may have been tiredness due to riding a bicycle to work in order to save streetcar fare, but more likely the tremor was caused by the neurological damage from the motorcycle accident, damage whose existence he continued to deny angrily even while trying to compensate for it. But whatever the cause, he never spilled the medicine. He might drop a glass, stumble over unseen objects, and carry on a losing battle with just about any machine with which he came in contact, but to my knowledge, my father never spilled those little sugar pills.

Did those pills really work? I haven't the scientific background to know. They seemed to. At times rather amazingly, though I suspect that sometimes we just got better. Regardless of their curative powers, sucking the little globules was infinitely comforting. Just hearing their Latinate names usually made me feel better: *Gelsemium, Aconite, Belladonna, Arnica, Ferrum Phos., Lachesis,* and the delightfully crude-sounding *Nux Vomica, "the student's remedy."* It was a litany of exotic sounds that lingered as pleasantly in the ear as their various tastes did on the tongue.

As an adult, I mostly steered clear of physicians of all persuasions, not convinced that homeopathy was everything my father thought, but certain that I'd rather avoid the eagerly advertised non-homeopathic pills and nostrums so many seemed to be taking. Once in a while though, when I went to my parents' for dinner, I'd offer my father a symptom or two, the way a guest might bring a bottle of wine or a bouquet of flowers.

"Wish I could do something about this rotten cold," I'd say. "Can't seem to shake it."

He'd brighten, promise to see what he could do, and later in the evening I'd hear him making a happy, musing sort of hum to himself as he delved into one of his homeopathic tomes. He'd read a bit, stick in a piece of paper to mark his place, and then reach for another book just to check out further possibilities. And before I left, he'd give me a dose and instructions on when and how many further doses should be taken and tell me to take the bottle home.

I'd thank him dutifully. Sometimes I remembered to take the follow-up doses; sometimes I didn't. But always I felt warmed, pleased to have given my father a chance to show his felt concern, so hard for him to express, and pleased to have shared a small moment that had little to do with medicine.

Since his death, I'll occasionally visit a doctor, but I'm apt to see just how long I can get by without any medication, preferring to let my fairly healthy hereditary constitution manage on its own.

There are, however, several little bottles in the drawer of our downstairs bathroom cabinet. *Arnica,* for garden variety bruises and sprains; *Hypericum,* which is the only thing I know of that seems to help little fingers caught in doors; *Rhus Tox,* for poison ivy; and a couple of others, not as neatly arranged as my father's, but they're there.

When I think back, I realize that the tightly packed shoe box represented order not only to me, but perhaps also to my father. We each have our own way of preserving order in our lives, and homeopathy, far more than just a medical exercise for my father, was perhaps a way of balancing, of helping him keep order among uncertainties, something that gave him a small measure of autonomy in a life governed by events over which he had little control.

Recently I discovered a small brown glass bottle with a black top labeled *Bryonia* in one of my dresser drawers. I don't know what it's given for and can't imagine how it got there. I held the bottle; it fit nicely in the hollow of my palm. I looked at the familiar buff-colored, red-and-black printed label and, after a moment, placed the bottle on the dresser, beside a picture.

Naomi Gladish Smith is a writer who lives in Glenview, Illinois. Her father was a Swedenborgian minister.

◆ **LEE F. SNYDER** ◆

The Letter

◆

HE CALLED US to his study. My father had something to say. It was Saturday and this gathering seemed as usual as ever. We had grown to expect that weekends were Dad's time to work on the house. He addressed domestic projects as he had his business: confront the problem, define it, attack it, and feel comfortable with your success. But Dad was hardly ever comfortable with his success. He shined when there was a problem and solved each with the same meticulous analysis. Success was an incidental byproduct of a game he had created and grown to love. It was a game at which he was the champion without any real competitors.

Now, as usual on Saturday, we were his work force. We replaced his employees. The only difference, the most important one, was that he could not fire us. I was fifteen before that fact hit me, and in my rebellious years, there were times when I tested the premise. After more than ten years of unquestioned following, a teenager's virus had supplanted my allegiance. I had learned to ask *why* and was seldom content with his answer. I've often wondered if the confused emotions of a teenaged male are not the unrecognized equivalent of menopause. My father understood my uneasiness and helped with patience.

There were always lists. Matter-of-fact assignments. Things that must get done. He would compose them at his desk, then subdivide and group them. Some were for me. Some were for my sister, Sarah. None was ever assigned to my mother. With her, they were always requests. She was his equal and often reminded him of that if he should ever slip and include her on his list. She had her own assignments and schedules. So, her involvement with his

Escher, Maurits Cornelis. *Three Worlds*. Lithograph, 1955. New York, Art Resource.

itineraries was always incidental. No less important. But they could never be assigned with the same impersonal dictation that we all knew to expect, and her inclusion in the meetings was made to look like afterthoughts. "Maybe if you have the time . . ." or "Do you think this is a good idea?"

After receiving an assignment I didn't want, I remember mumbling once about what he would have done if I'd never been born. Dad thought for a moment and, without lifting his head from the list to address me, he suggested that it was probably too late to reverse the situation. But, if I insisted, I should present it as a formal request to my mother. Mother frowned. Sarah giggled, and I did the work.

It wasn't that he enjoyed giving us things to do. It was just the way he organized. "This has to be done. We'll all take a part and do it faster and better than any one of us could ever do it alone." With Dad, the whole was always greater than the sum of the parts.

It was March. The remnants of the winter's snow production magnified the sunshine. Red buds had begun forming on the maple trees outside the study window. We all had our own ways of getting through these meetings. Sarah usually sat in the corner of the sofa and grabbed a pillow. She would adjust and readjust the stuffing throughout the meeting. Mother sat quietly listening to what Dad had to say, adding things as necessary. She would remind him of fine points he may have overlooked. I watched the maple trees and the bird feeder as the chickadees moved in and out of view.

There was never a fire in the fireplace at these meetings. Mother used to say, "Fires shouldn't be made until the evening when the sun can't compete with the orange glow." Dad's reasoning dealt with the efficiency of the moment. "Let's get this over quickly," he'd say. "Fires demand your attention." And then he'd add: "Oceans roar and we watch. Cars roar and we watch. Fires roar too." Dad seldom roared.

His desk was "unusually busy"—his way of explaining an out-of-character mess. There was one piece of paper neatly centered in front of him as I walked in. He calmly put the pen down as my sister entered the room and settled into the couch. She was the last of us to find time for this small interruption. As he rose from his chair behind the desk, he covered the paper with yesterday's mail. He was slow to make eye contact with me, carefully moving around the desk to his favorite chair. There was a grunt as he fell into it and sank comfortably. His smile was apologetic.

He spoke to us now in the most concise terms. It was his way. The words formed slowly finding a place on his tongue. They rolled past his lips accompanied by an appropriate exhalation of air and the sweet sound of his voice. The three items combined to give meaning to his facial expressions. The sentences had structure. His face showed purpose. They came as thoughts and phrases and then final words. He had been sick. He had gone to see the doctor a month before. He'd told none of us. The tests had generated some concern and more tests with them. The words continued to flow. They rolled from his lips and through the air to our ears, then our minds, to rest on our hearts. He had terminal cancer. Six months, maybe a year.

I didn't hear much else for the next hour. The feeling of danger mixed with hopelessness had washed over me. My ears pounded with the sounds of an accelerated heartbeat. I sensed my mother's panic as she held him and wept silently into his shoulder. Sarah never moved. The shock on her face was washed in tear-stained lines. She pressed the pillow tightly in her arms with her knees a part of the embrace.

There were seven months left. Just seven, nearly to the day. That October Saturday after his death, I stood at the study window near his desk when Sarah walked in. We had both cried enough over the last few weeks. No crying now.

Dad had always said autumn shouldn't be thought of as the end of summer or even a preparation for winter. Despite its identity with the seasonal cycle, he said, fall has a unique character all its own—"a beauty unequaled by any other time. The colors are like no other season with weather that challenges the senses." The maples were blazing this day: red, orange, and yellow.

His death wasn't easy for him or for us. But he prepared for it the same way he prepared each of his days. He prepared things for us too. He tried to ensure that the only thing missing from our lives after his departure would be him.

Sarah sat rocking in his desk chair looking at the page on the desk, the same paper he fumbled over that day we shared his news. Weeks before, mother had rearranged his things, a sort of preparation that would guarantee his return. The work helped her face his passing. As a final act, she centered the paper on the desk clearing everything else away. We had all read and memorized it. It stayed on the desk for several months before mother laid it between the pages of one of his volumes on Jefferson.

For all his lists and firm guidance, my father never had a lesson to teach. Teaching was incidental—by example. I learned from him because I admired him and wanted to be like him. If there is a lesson, it is that our time here is set in a series of events within a larger cycle. All events are like the seasons with their own beginnings and endings, and all people experience joy and pain as natural, unavoidable byproducts. The cycles, like the seasons, are inevitable; it is the emotion we bring to them that varies. The beauty in each may be interpreted differently; only the value each of us places on the beauty changes—the intensity of the colors and brightness of the leaves. If we are lucky, we experience a range of emotions that, by design or otherwise, balance the good with the bad.

Death is as much a part of the cycle as life, maybe more. As the ultimate confrontation, death is the mechanism that forces us through the cycle's end to assess the value of that which has gone. As the element completing the cycle, death confirms the sense of order and allows us to accept the cycle and recognize its identity.

I can't claim a change in my life came with his passing, though his absence was significant. I'm nearly as old as he was when he talked to us that day. I'm healthy, reasonably happy, and secure. I occasionally bite my nails. I sometimes get up late. My car is often more dirty than clean. But there is always purpose in what I do, and, above all else, I try to do it well: confront, define, attack, and feel comfortable with my success. That sense of order was his gift, and the one I have passed on to my children.

He had a different way of explaining it. My father's letter to us was printed on the paper—the one guarded by Jefferson. It was his final guidance: "Being happy with what you are and who you've become should never be the life goal. It should be an accident of your being. Order brings contentment, and contentment security." And, almost as an afterthought, "Never forget me."

Just as the words of his illness choked us all that day; just as he eloquently inserted that emotional storm among us; so had he given us the privilege of sharing his cycle. There was pain in his passing—verification of his worth to those left behind. If we are lucky, it is pain that others will feel for us when we go.

Lee F. Snyder is a professional nature photographer, writer, and knowledgeable bird-watcher.

PETER BETHANIS

Ice Fishing

◆

NO MATTER WHAT OUR SCHEDULES, my father and I set aside one week each year, just before the January thaw, to travel to our cabin in the one-general-store town of Guerette, Maine. As soon as the pickup turns onto the dirt road that weaves eight miles into the woods, the pressures of daily working life seem to ease up a bit, if only for a week.

After our many years of venturing to the cabin, it is still amazing to wake up the first morning and gaze out the big picture window that overlooks the frozen lake. Just as when I was a boy, the ice shacks remind me of hats strewn across the snow. In the warmth of the cast-iron barrel that my father converted into a wood stove, we eat scrambled eggs and bacon at the oak table.

Outside the cabin, the cold pierces my face. We load augers, jigs, traps, and the milk carton of bait into the wooden sleds hooked up to the snowmobiles. My father reminds me to get the ladles to scoop up the slush the augers make around the edges of the holes. I thud a snowball above the door of the shed and watch him duck inside for more traps. Then I whip the cord that shocks the snowmobile to life.

The morning sun spreads across the vast whiteness, and I have to squint to slide the wriggling smelt on the hook. The tiny fish darts like a threaded needle through the black hole, out of sight. From a distance I can see my father twist the auger like a corkscrew into the ice. I begin another hole and turn the handle around until my arms burn. I love how the revolving blade grinds up slivers of ice and all at once breaks through, sending water rushing over my rubber boots.

Olivier, Leah. *Salmo salar sebago*. Pencil, 1995.

Once the holes are drilled and the flags are locked, there is nothing to do but wait. We sit out of the wind behind the snowmobiles, the thought of a red flag popping up filling every blood vessel.

A few years ago, a flag had sprung up, signaling a catch. I stumbled in my sluggish boots over slush and knelt down over the trap. The spool of line was unraveling so fast, the trap was shaking. In hopes of tiring the fish, I let the line uncoil. My stomach churning, I removed the trap from over the hole. Tugging the line, I felt the weight of the fish.

By this time, my father had trudged to the hole and knelt down to get a closer look. The string bunched up in frozen snarls as I dragged the heavy weight closer and closer to the open mouth in the ice.

When the fish appeared from below the surface, my father and I glanced at one another in disbelief. The salmon was too large to pull up through the hole I heard a blur of comments from my father in the background. In one quick jerk, I pulled the thrashing salmon halfway up through the hole, and as I hefted the slick body, its flashing jaw broke free. My father jammed his arm down the frozen tunnel all the way up to his shoulder, and for a moment briefer than a few seconds, clutched the immense fish—until the frigid water took hold of his expression, and he pulled up his empty hand.

Usually on a good day, we will catch our limit of two trout and two salmon apiece. We have never come close in size to the iron-jawed monster that slipped between our fingers that day.

When dusk comes, the fish stop biting. Lined in the snow, their lethargic gills suck in the air. Pulling in the traps, the wind freezes the water to my hands until they turn numb, and I cannot feel the hooks stick into the flesh. Then we rope the fish through the gills to the inside of the wooden sleds.

On the ride home across the lake, our snowmobiles hum like wasps through the darkness as the engines rumble over the ice. Sometimes we race the snowmobiles until the speed forms tears that freeze to our eyelids.

Back at the cabin, I sit out on the deck and slit open the white belly of each fish, yank out hankies of trout guts, clean their insides with snow until my fingers turn raw and pink. Alone with the task of cleaning fish, I watch the orange disk of sun lower beneath the thin strip of pines that divides lake and sky; then I collect all the remains and spread them out in the snow in a pile for the raccoons.

In the evening, the lantern spreads a mild glow inside the cabin. Our stomachs are filled with the feathers of white meat. We listen to the wind whip invisible hands across the windows' dark glass. My father, his face older than I have ever seen it, sits in his chair as he strains his eyes to untangle lines in the traps.

Deep in the night, I grope down the long dark path to the lake with a bucket in each hand. Then I break open the thin skin of ice already beginning to film over an old entrance into the lake. Carefully, I scoop up the water we'll heat over the stove for our baths.

Out on the lake at night the sky is huge and open around me, twitching with more stars than I could possibly fathom in a lifetime. Just before I lug the heavy buckets back to the cabin, I stand alone under the stars on the silent table of ice, and, for the first time in a year, I am able to put things in their proper perspective.

Peter Bethanis received an MFA in English at the University of Massachusetts at Amherst. His poetry and essays have appeared in *County Journal, Blueline, The Indianpolis Star,* and elsewhere. He currently teaches English composition at Butler University.

O'Keeffe, Georgia. *Red Canna*. Oil on canvas mounted on masonite, ca. 1923. Tucson: The University of Arizona Museum of Art. Gift of Oliver James.

♦ *JOHN L. HITCHCOCK* ♦

Meaning Out of Chaos

♦

OUR WORLD IS PATTERNED AND COMPLEX—unpredictable, yet unified. These qualities, as applied to physical systems, are studied in the new branch of mathematical physics known as chaos theory. We can draw upon those explorations in physics to find metaphors for qualities of human living and our quest for meaning.

Each human act has meaning, even if we are unaware of it, and that meaning links the act to persons and events. To the extent that we can become conscious of the meanings more fully, we are more alive, more purposeful, and more fulfilled. Not that we could live without sheer impulse; sometimes our very lives depend on it. But the more we see of the interrelatedness and infinity of all things, the more we are in touch with an awe which is essential to who we are. In fact, if we could live in awe, we would be satisfied with every moment of our lives.

Mystical systems often inspire awe, as does the sense of the miraculous in general. We desire to be lifted "out of the mundane," the dreary, the sheer everydayness of it all. Yet, the patterns we could see, the numinosity we could experience, even by sitting down to contemplate a square foot of ground, are usually lost to us. The true gift of living lies in seeing "the universe in a grain of sand, eternity in an hour," as William Blake put it. For this seeing, what is most often needed is a transformation of attitude and not some sort of specialized training.

That we easily lose sight of patterns of meaning which are present in the world and in our acts is due, on the one hand, to the fact that they are subtle, and on the other to the fact that they will only show themselves *under certain conditions*.

We must be ready to choose to attend to them, but that readiness does not depend on any esoteric spiritual discipline. It usually has more to do with how much pain has entered one's life, for if pain has its right effect, it softens us and opens us to what we have been missing. It counteracts the reckless speed with which we pursue our egocentric goals.

Chaos theory has a lot to say about effects which are subtle and about the opening up of possibilities. I want to expand here on just one idea drawn from images in that field—that of opening ourselves to perceive that which is subtle, patterned, and meaningful. We often say that this perception is the province of the artist. That level of seeing, however, is not only *open* to all of us, it is *required* of us in the very nature of things. We are indeed able to bring about the conditions under which we can see for ourselves the patterns of meaning.

There are a few metaphors related to chaos theory, which I have found helpful in seeing more deeply into the meanings available to us at every moment. In part, I have been pushed in the direction of new metaphors by my own inability to meditate or to pray in the usual sense of those words. Perhaps some readers also have felt an emptiness in attempting what appears to be so natural to others. I prefer to look at it, however, as something *creative* blocking those more usual paths for us so that we are forced to seek other means of fulfilling what we have sought through meditation.

Subtle Possibilities

PICTURE IN YOUR MIND, if you will, a new-born child, and imagine all of the potentials present in that new being. If we think about it, we usually envision something lofty and creative—something that helps humanity at large and which also yields individual satisfaction. Sometimes we can see a specific talent shine through early in the child's life, though our society has a remarkable propensity to stifle originality through socialization.

Actually, this imaginative exercise holds a danger which we need to keep in mind but which may also help us to discover our own untapped reserves: often, we will project onto a child those potentials which are unfulfilled in ourselves. Make a list, then, of all the qualities or gifts which occurred to you in the imagination, and ask yourself if any of them might apply to you, apart from your fears of approaching them.

To continue the original thread of thought, if we look objectively at humanity as a whole, such potentials as we visualize as present at birth are not usually actualized to the full. What, then, might it take to realize them? External conditions should be favorable, of course, with family support and understanding and with good mentors in all areas of daily life. Yet, that is not enough. Any capacity for originality will only be fulfilled if something in the person perceives the capacity, desires the possible achievements, and inwardly takes hold to direct the efforts to that end. External encouragement and training may well play a helpful part, but the creativity itself is internal to the individual; nothing external can force it to come to fruition.

We are complex and unpredictable beings, which are qualities parallel to those that are studied in chaos theory. Complex systems contain or embody points of energy balance, known as "singular points." When the rate at which energy flows in the system reaches a singular point, possibilities for the use of that energy increase unlimitedly. A singular point is a threshold for an entire new vista of potential happenings, as when one climbs out of a deep valley onto a high plain, with many possible directions on the new level.

The conditions under which the possibilities multiply without limit constitute the meaning of the term "chaos," and the tangle of new possibilities is known as the "foam," because one can't tell what path one actually is on. At least, the ego can't! Something greater does indeed know. The question is whether the ego can tune in to the deeper meaning.

At singular points, a very small force from a more subtle, wider ranging patterning can decide which course a system will take. The great nineteenth-century physicist, James Clerk Maxwell commented on this situation:

> In all such cases there is one common circumstance—the system has a quantity of potential energy, which is capable of being transformed into motion, but which cannot begin to be so transformed till the system has reached a certain configuration, to attain which requires an expenditure of work, which in certain cases may be infinitesimally small, and in general bears no definite proportion to the energy

developed in consequence thereof. For example, the rock loosed by frost and balanced on a singular point of the mountainside, the little spark which kindles the great forest, the little word which sets the world a-fighting, the little scruple which prevents one from doing his own will, the little spore which blights all the potatoes, the little gemmule which makes us philosophers or idiots. Every existence above a certain rank has its singular points: the higher the rank, the more of them. At these points, influences whose physical magnitude is too small to be taken account of by a finite being, may produce results of the greatest importance. All great results produced by human endeavor depend on taking advantage of these singular states when they occur.

The fact that tiny amounts of energy can change the entire course of events for a system in the "foam" at a singular point, gives us the hint that if our own consciousness can perceive the subtle influences on our psyches, we can indeed participate in what I call the greater Patterning of things, the evolution of meaning in our lives.

Maxwell is speaking of systems which somehow get loaded with unused energy, such as the buildup of dead wood on the floor of a forest, which then can be touched off with a tiny spark. We are far from knowing all of the forms in which spiritual energy is stored, but we see a negative form of it released in riots, which corresponds well to the forest fire. In our individual lives, our unfulfilled patterns of wholeness lead to unused potential energy in our psyches, often in the form of great buried anger. The trick is to produce a symbol which will release the energy creatively.

Slowing Down

WHAT THIS REQUIRES OF US in awareness is often a quieting down, rather than a building up of energy. The singular point, the place of creative instability and opening possibility, most often in us must be reached by lowering our ego–will energy level, rather than by raising it, not to mention our ego-protective energy, or egocentricity, which must be subdued even prior to working on the ego–will. The energy can then restructure itself in a meaning-pattern deeper in our psyche. When the ego is functioning properly, we can indeed become aware of the changes.

There is a nice analogy to this quieting down in the case of the formation of an atom. The simplest chemical element is hydrogen, whose atom consists of one proton (as its nucleus), and one electron. If an electron is moving too fast, having too much energy, the proton can't capture it, just as if one wanted to put a bullet into a cardboard box, by shooting the bullet at the box with a gun. The bullet would pass right through, without "seeing" or "feeling" the box at all. One must bring them together gently.

It is the same with our lives. We live like bullets fired from guns, and we don't see or feel the more subtle patterns to which we might be related.

The analogy has another beautiful point, based on the wave-particle duality in the nature of every elementary entity. The high-speed electron acts as a *particle,* that is, as something detached from everything else. When it slows down, permitting it to feel the presence of the proton and to become "bound" to it, the electron manifests its *wave* nature and shows a wide variety of patterns, which it cannot do when it is "free." The much more massive proton acts as an anchor for this patterning of the electron.

In our lives as well, when we are, in a sense, free as egos, we are detached beings; but if we can quiet our ego energy, or ego demands, and permit ourselves to be bound to something greater as an anchor, we participate in the greater Patterning, which confers much deeper meaning on our lives. I am not here referring to a social collective as the greater something, but rather to the roots of our own human wholeness. When it becomes bound to the atom, making a whole, the electron makes a transition to a state in which its own inherent patterns are brought to concrete being. It is the same with us. The potential patterns are not only seen via the quieting and bonding process; they come to a new level of being.

The message I am developing is that we can indeed perceive and be guided by the source of greater meaning, giving our lives a new spiritual anchor. The anchor I have in mind, however, is not any fixed system. It is not external at all, but internal. The question then becomes: What can awaken in us the desire to find this spiritual center within ourselves and bind ourselves to it? What will turn us toward a spiritual anchoring? We will return to this question after building a fuller picture of the subtle field.

We have encountered the idea of a field of subtle forces which can influence the direction a system can take at the singular points in the foam of possibility. Our normal ego-consciousness is, in a sense, too "high powered" for us to perceive this field, which means, in part, that our normal consciousness is very partial, very limited, and that there is an entire world to be explored.

Prigogine (1984) points out that experiments with certain chemical systems show that at singular points a new and deeper order is likely to exert its influence based on more subtle forces which he calls "long-range correlations." This is the basis for the title of his book, *Order Out of Chaos*. When systems are in the chaotic foam, the deeper order can emerge by means of a communication which comes from a wider field of subtle patterning. This deeper order is indeed felt at first by our egos as a limitation, or straightening, but it is the ultimate source of meaning for our lives. It is a *creative spiritual patterning*, especially in view of the fact that creativity can and often does occur at singular points.

In creativity, meaning is revealed. Let us briefly explore the roots of creativity, as envisioned in terms of chaos theory.

Finitude and Creativity

OUR CREATIVITY is closely linked to the fact that we are finite, that we encounter limits. These limitations also make us as complex as we are, giving us the characteristic known in chaos theory as being "non-linear," which makes us swerve and turn. To be linear is to be predictable. Unpredictability is the very meaning of chaos in chaos theory, but it is *fertile:* limitations force us to be creative.

We may think or feel, for instance, that the fact that we have limited lifespans, i.e., that we die, is a defect in the design of the universe, or of the vision of the Creator. The fact that we die is central to who we are. A being that did not encounter such a limitation need not expend any creativity in relating to the meaning of death, which is such a profound reality for us and the wellspring for so much human struggle in every arena of the spirit.

We might even note that the evolution of physiological systems leading to human beings can be visualized as a series of creative, patterned responses to a changing environment full of limitations. Thus, the whole of our being and functioning is rooted in finitude.

If you think about it, virtually all of our creativity is problem solving at some level—a response to limitation. A being that encounters no obstacles needs no creativity; it is not a value. If we find meaning in death, in effort, in overcoming obstacles, in achievement, we might even say that meaning is rooted in finitude.

One of the frustrations of being human is often the very fact that we are finite that we cannot accomplish all we wish, or even intend, to do. But without limitations, there would be no need for creativity. It's amazing how much we can indeed put together in our lives when we are required to improvise. Even the notion of a *fulfilled* life has no meaning without death. I say this in the hope that we will be moved to explore the meaning of psychic death and rebirth, for the fulfillment of our lives. This will mean choosing to retreat from the clamor and demands of the ego for its own protection and to begin to try to attend to the true possibilities of the soul.

Creativity occurs at the singular points, where possibilities open up in the chaotic foam. Creativity also is the positive response to limitation.

We generally experience beauty through finite forms, and artists also experience their creativity in solving problems posed by their medium. Poets often love the challenge of writing within specific poetic forms. Genius and inspiration find new patterns within limitation. In artistic creation (whatever the level of expression), we are actively drawing on the subtle field of which we have been speaking.

Where there is little experience of feeling and responding to the influence of the subtle patterning, we can still use our vision of possibility as the basis for our action. If we can slow down, as the electron slows down, we can experience our own patterning as that given from the wider source which is the ground of our being.

The Patterning Field

THE FIELD, also known as the world-field, is a neutral term for the creative Patterning which has guided the whole of evolution. Inspired by the ancient Chinese Tao Te Ching, we might say: Without form, it is the source of all form. Without being visible, it is the source of everything which can be seen. Without doing, it is the shaper and guide of all that is and all that happens.

The typical ego doesn't easily accept knowledge of the field, for that knowledge threatens its sense of security and self-sufficiency. Only feeling the field as a fact can provide the needed motivation and the solid ground which the ego needs in order to move and change. Most of us have had at least some experience of feeling the field at work in our lives. Perhaps a job turns up unexpectedly, or a person, or even an object, but in a way which seems miraculous or destined. Even the expression "turns up" comes from games with cards, where chance or something more is at work. We say that something's moving, or that we're "on a roll." At other times, it's exceedingly difficult to trust the field for help. At such times we may have to go forward on the trust that such occurrences are real; that is, we may have to *choose* to live that way, when times feel chaotic. At least then we know that we are living from within. This recognition is at least a part of what can turn us toward the new spiritual anchoring described earlier.

In science, a field is something which can exert a force on matter and move it around, as a magnetic field can move bits of iron. We can visualize such physical fields as the magnetic field as the *physical* components of the total world-field. However, there are also psychic and spiritual fields as components of the same total world-field. We can calculate and measure physical fields. The others are harder to get hold of, but one example of a psychic field is personal charisma, so potent in certain persons. Another is the mass psyche of a mob. Acknowledging the reality of these fields can help us to know the world-field more personally.

In chaos theory, every point of space and time in a system is in touch with a centralizing field, known as a "strange attractor," if the energy flow puts the system concerned in the chaotic foam. It is a *guiding* field, which evolves the system's conditions unpredictably, within limits. The world-field, including the psychic–spiritual field, seems to possess similar qualities. It, too, is a centralizing field which guides each of us on a spiritual path that is unique to every individual.

That center remains with us, wherever we are, but we remain unconscious of it, unless we choose to be present to it and to trust it in our new intention.

Psychologist Erich Neumann called this presence and our trust in it the opening of ourselves to "field-knowledge," which is distinguished from ego-knowledge, and he named the overall effect of the field over time "centroversion." Ego knowledge functions in terms of contrasts which make figures stand out from the ground within which we are seeing. Ego knowledge is "contrast-knowledge." We may speak of the field as functioning *beyond* contrast-knowledge, but really it is the *foundation,* even of our ego-consciousness, the ultimate ground of the figure, so to speak, the realm of things as they are in themselves. To refer to an example used earlier, an electron in its *wholeness* resides in the field, while we *see* it by means of the contrast of wave and particle. The electron in its wholeness is the ground of what we perceive in terms of its dual aspects. In order to touch the field psychologically, we must be near a singular point, an unstable equilibrium, or a creative balance in the tension of opposites. James Hillman (1979, p.14) points out that we need to become aware of, and accept, our ambivalences. He says that "ambivalence is the adequate reaction of the whole psyche to whole truths." We must learn to accept, and even to love, our ambivalences, for if we can hold to the tension, the "third point," a new birth can occur for us and lead us onward in life. The *work of acceptance* is something at which we can be active, and it is what I refer to as a new kind of meditation. One of my teachers, Elizabeth Boyden Howes, put it as, "You are centered if you can go either way," which gives a good image, both of creative ambivalence and the readiness to act for whichever value from the greater field tips the balance of our response in the inner and outer situation.

The work of acceptance of our ambivalences, accepting ourselves as we are, not complacently, but as a point from which to proceed, is part of a larger work of accepting the world as it is. This may sound simple, but not when we know that the unpredictability, the built-in chaotic nature of complex systems, throws the responsibility for conscious seeking of the spiritual center right back in our laps. The Patterning confers meaning, but it is not a fixed plan;

the outcomes are unknown and depend on us. To accept that is to stand up and move on our journeys, as it were, on our own.

Experiencing Meaning

WE MUST ASK OURSELVES whether our primary experience of ourselves is as separated, even alienated, as a cut-off single particle, or whether we also know the creative Patterning and the gifts it offers us. It is up to us to realize when we are moving "faster than a speeding bullet," and to know that there is another way. Our acceptance *by* reality is predicated only on our acceptance *of* reality. In a sense, we signal our part of the bargain when we deliberately slow down, in order to seek beyond what we know as contrast-knowledge and to seek direction by the field from within. As with the electron, our pattern comes to concrete being when we permit ourselves to be anchored by that which is greater *within.*

It is through our own unique patterning that we integrate ourselves into the greater Patterning. To discover our own patterning, we must become quiet enough to permit it to show its form. When we do, we are aware of being anchored in the whole of things.

It may well be unfamiliar ground for a long time, but in the end there is no other value to hold to which gives life the same satisfaction. We become bound when we so choose from the heart. As psychologist C.G. Jung said:

> In the last analysis every life is a realization of a whole, that is, of a Self, for which reason this realization can also be called individuation. All life is bound to individual carriers who realize it, and it is simply inconceivable without them. But every carrier is charged with an individual destiny and destination, and the realization of these alone makes sense of life. (Jung, CW12, paragraph no. 330)

Our ego-consciousness has indeed given us our freedom, along with our ego-detachment. What it comes to now is to accept the straightening of the field, while putting the freedom to work in service of the greater Patterning by choice.

Creativity is ours, as well, if we can open ourselves to it. Many artists and composers consciously give over to the field in their creative work. Creativity is in each thing and each person as a representative of the God-center that is everywhere present. What we carry with us, wherever we go, becomes more widely visible as a much fuller reality, if we look. We usually look at the behavior of others still without seeing the whole person, much less seeing the God-center within the other. If we would imagine each human as we do a newborn child, our compassion would be aroused for all the unfulfillment we witness each day, and for ourselves as well.

Meaning is as difficult to define as love. There certainly are shared human circumstances which are widely felt as significant, but as with the appreciation of art, in the end we are responsible for the experience of meaning. There is a sense of rightness, and the feeling of numinosity. Terms such as self-realization and fulfillment are useful (meaningful), even when dark acts fulfill themselves in disaster. Finding and living from our own individual patterning, whatever the cost, is the real ground of meaning in our lives. For that, the ego must be strong in commitment to the process but must also sacrifice its priority as to will. Its energy must be tamed.

I have been presenting ways of looking at the unfolding of life out of the chaotic unpredictability which really gives rise to life itself. It seems that there is a new focus on human inwardness, as an organ of creativity in the cosmos. This inwardness redefines who we are, and our responsibility for the actualization of meaning. Though our intentionality carries a new burden, the potential reward is also new—a new aliveness. As with love, meaning is not solely for the individual, in spite of individual responsibility. We create a world by listening to a world-field which encompasses us all, and the rightness is really there only if the whole is enhanced. We can choose to participate in that work.

John L. Hitchcock, a physicist–astronomer who works in the field of science and religion, is the author of *Atoms, Snowflakes & God: The Covergence of Science and Religion* (Quest Books, 1986), and *The Web of the Universe: Jung, the New Physics, and Human Spirituality* (Paulist Press, 1991). The latter is part of the Paulist Press series, *Jung and Spirituality*. His third book, *The New Labyrinth: Images of Spirituality from Chaos Theory,* is under consideration for publication. He is revising a fourth book: *Revisioning the Cosmos with the Heart.*

EDWARD BARATTA

Physical Devotions

♦

Bolt the door and raise the shades;
allow the light to tumble in alive.

Of all things superfluous, clear the desk,
the wooden duck with pens that don't work.

A cup of tea in the left hand, square
the back against a thick, oak chair,

and listen: music of Bach floats in from
the apartment above, nothing one can

or would want to do to stop that. Rugs
are swept, the sink is scrubbed, and

the empty white space that threatened us
now bears witness to our courage.

Edward Baratta's poetry has been published in numerous journals, including *Harvard Review, Poetry East, The Massachusetts Review,* and *The Literary Review*. Recent dramatic recitations have been given at First Church in Cambridge, Congregational, and the Cambridge Bach Ensemble. Edward dedicates this poem to Scott Metcalfe, the Ensemble director.

Swedenborg Foundation

The mission of the Swedenborg Foundation is to foster an affirmative, adventurous, and increasingly broad engagement with the theological thought of Emanuel Swedenborg, especially among persons desiring to apply spiritual principles to life.
—Board of Directors, 1989

The Swedenborg Foundation has been a publisher of the theological works of Emanuel Swedenborg since 1849. We also publish a diverse selection of books, such as this one, under the imprint of Chrysalis Books. The purpose of these titles is to convey to a contemporary audience the relevance of Swedenborg's ideas.

We invite you to join us in a lively engagement of spiritual process. The insights of the eighteenth-century Swedish visionary are both inspiring and timely to today's reader. On the next page you will find a selection of books that help make Swedenborg's writings more accessible and useful. You may also call or write us for a complete catalog of publications.

Light in My Darkness
Helen Keller
Revised by Ray Silverman / Preface by Norman Vincent Peale
A powerful look into the world of ideas that shaped Helen Keller's faith. She drew inspiration from the writings of Emanuel Swedenborg, a spiritual resource she called "light in my darkness, the voice in my silence."
5 1/2 x 8 1/2, paperback, 184 pages, photographs, ISBN 0-87785-146-8, $9.95

Angels in Action: What Swedenborg Saw and Heard
Robert H. Kirven
For a period of twenty-seven years, Emanuel Swedenborg talked with angels and spirits. The author draws from Swedenborg's writings and his own personal experience to show how angels work with us from birth through death and how we can be angels on earth.
5 1/2 x 8 1/2, papeback, 128 pages, illustrations, ISBN 0-87785-147-6, $8.95

A Scientist Explores Spirit: A Compact Biography of Emanuel Swedenborg, with Key Concepts of Swedenborg's Theology
George F. Dole and Robert H. Kirven
A lively, concise introduction to the life and thought of Emanuel Swedenborg, focusing on the tension between scientific and spiritual interests.   5 1/2 x 8 1/2, paperback, 104 pages, ISBN 0-87785-143-3, $9.95

Swedenborg's View from Within
Translated with commentary by George F. Dole
Modern translations of key passages from Swedenborg, with helpful explanations of Swedenborg's ideas by the translator.
5 1/2 x 8 1/2, paperback, 192 pages, ISBN 0-87785-148-4, $11.95

Testimony to the Invisible, and Other Essays on Swedenborg
Edited by James Lawrence
A selection of essays about Swedenborg by such great writers as Jorgé Luis Borges, Czeslaw Milosz, D. T. Suzuki, and Colin Wilson, among others.   5 1/2 x 8 1/2, paperback, 200 pages, ISBN 0-87785-149-2, $11.95

Call **(800) 355-3222** to place an order or request a catalog, or write:
Swedenborg Foundation/P.O. Box 549/West Chester, Pennsylvania 19381.